W9-CMP-566

DISCARD
RETIRÉ

Canadian pageant

THE LINK BETWEEN THE OCEANS

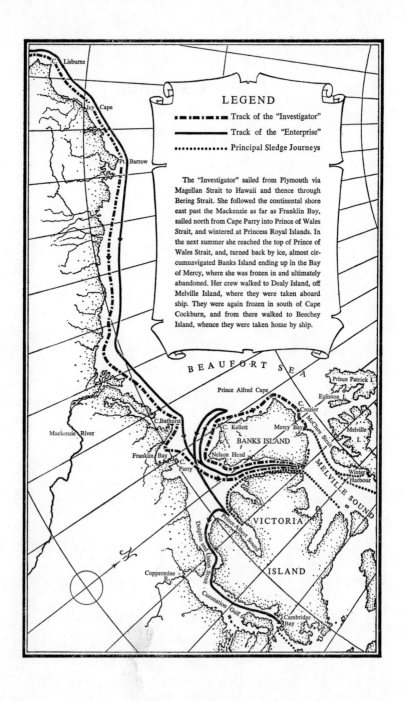

LEGEND

▪━ ▪━ ▪━ ▪ Track of the "Investigator"
━━━━━━━━ Track of the "Enterprise"
•••••••••••• Principal Sledge Journeys

The "Investigator" sailed from Plymouth via Magellan Strait to Hawaii and thence through Bering Strait. She followed the continental shore east past the Mackenzie as far as Franklin Bay, sailed north from Cape Parry into Prince of Wales Strait, and wintered at Princess Royal Islands. In the next summer she reached the top of Prince of Wales Strait, and, turned back by ice, almost circumnavigated Banks Island ending up in the Bay of Mercy, where she was frozen in and ultimately abandoned. Her crew walked to Dealy Island, off Melville Island, where they were taken aboard ship. They were again frozen in south of Cape Cockburn, and from there walked to Beechey Island, whence they were taken home by ship.

C. Lisburne
Icy Cape
Pt. Barrow

BEAUFORT SEA

Prince Alfred Cape
Prince Patrick I.
Eglinton I.
C. Crozier
McClure Strait
Melville I.
C. Bathurst
C. Kellett
Mercy Bay
Mackenzie River
BANKS ISLAND
Winter Harbour
Franklin Bay
Nelson Head
MELVILLE SOUND
C. Parry
VICTORIA
Dolphin and Union Strait
Prince Albert Sound
Coppermine R.
ISLAND
Coronation Gulf
Cambridge Bay

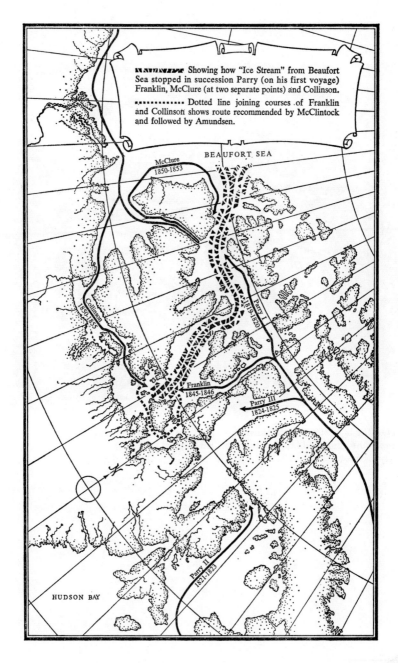

Showing how "Ice Stream" from Beaufort Sea stopped in succession Parry (on his first voyage) Franklin, McClure (at two separate points) and Collinson.

.... Dotted line joining courses of Franklin and Collinson shows route recommended by McClintock and followed by Amundsen.

BEAUFORT SEA

McClure
1850-1853

Collinson
1850-1853

Parry I
1819-1820

Franklin
1845-1846

Parry III
1824-1825

Parry II
1821-1823

HUDSON BAY

Maps

" Then the biggest advanced slowly towards us, whilst his four
companions remained huddled together. He stopped at
thirty paces . . . ."

LESLIE H. NEATBY

The Link between the Oceans

 Longmans, Green and Company, Toronto

To the memory of

KENNETH WILLIAM NEATBY

1900–1958

Naught of ill can touch him any more,

And glorious rest he hath from many toils.

  Euripides

Copyright © 1960

Copyright Canada 1960

by L. H. Neatby

All rights reserved

Longmans, Green and Company

20 Cranfield Road, Toronto 16

First edition 1960

Designed by Arnold Rockman, MTDC

Illustration by Kenneth Saltmarche

Maps by Douglas Baker

Printed and bound in Canada

by the Hunter Rose Co. Limited

Contents

64-2665

Preface

A HUNDRED AND thirty years ago the north shore of
Canada and the seas and islands beyond were a forbidding
and mysterious region of which nothing was clearly known. The
map did not extend so far. A British seaman, Sir John Franklin,
sailed into these ice-strewn seas by canoe and did much to
give northern Canada a shape. As everyone knows, he tried his
luck too far, and perished with all his men in an attempt to
find the "link between the oceans", the Northwest Passage. Many
ships sailed, year after year, to search for the lost men; and on
one of these was a German missionary from Labrador. When he
came home he published the story of his adventures in
German. A shortened French edition was published a year later,
and on the latter (along with English works by Dr. Alexander
Armstrong and Captain Sherard Osborn) this book is based. It
tells the story of Captain McClure and the *Investigator*.

The search for Franklin in which McClure and his men played
so large a part unfolded the map of the islands to a latitude five
hundred miles north of the Canadian mainland. But it did more
than that. It proved that long journeys on the polar ice-caps
were possible, and opened the way for Peary and Shackleton,
for Amundsen and Scott, whose exploits are the glory of the
twentieth century. All who love true stories of adventure are
thankful that the North and South Poles were discovered by men
who travelled on foot, before the airplane and the snow-cat
had taken the sporting element out of such enterprises. The credit
for that belongs to the pioneers of the Canadian Arctic, and
not least of all to the brave young German who tells his story
in the following pages.

Chapter one

A landsman sets sail

O N A C H I L L and windy January morning more than a hundred years ago, a strange sight was to be seen in Plymouth harbour. Two ships had just cast off their moorings and dropped away from the dock. There they lay in midstream, while boats that had delivered the last letters and parting gifts backed clear and pulled towards the shore.

A stranger who knew anything of the sea would have wondered at what he saw. The two vessels flew the ensign of the British Navy, but in structure and equipment were as unlike men-of-war as any ships could be. They were bluff in the bow, broad in the beam, and their upper decks were loaded with a queer assortment of freight—casks, crates, sledges, and ice-saws, all securely lashed into place, but hampering the deck in a way that would not have been tolerated on a regular ship of war. Looking more closely, our stranger would observe that bumpers of hardwood and iron were fastened to bow and stern of both ships, and that heavy planking, running the full length of the water-line, was bolted to their sides.

Suddenly a boat pulled swifty towards the departing ships. Signals from the boat were replied to from one of the ships; the boat drew alongside, and as she heaved up and down, a man, tall and athletic but plainly no seaman, scrambled up the side and was courteously helped on board. His chest was hoisted up after him.

Both ships' sails began to draw, and they were off. They received and answered the salutes of the warships at the harbour mouth, rounded the breakwater, and under a low grey sky were soon lost to view among the rollers and whitecaps of the English

Channel. What were they, on what errand were they bound with those fantastic cargoes, and who was the queer-looking landsman who joined them at the last moment?

The two vessels were Her Majesty's Ships *Enterprise* and *Investigator,* off to write the last chapter but one in the longest and most exciting of the tales of the sea. The odd-looking passenger was John A. Miertsching, a simple-minded German missionary, whom chance had made a temporary officer of the British Navy. To understand what that accident was, we must look back three hundred years to the very beginning of Canadian history.

As soon as Columbus discovered the New World, English and French sailors began to look for a short route to China by some channel through the new continent or around its northern end. John Cabot searched the shores of Newfoundland and Nova Scotia for an opening; Jacques Cartier groped his way into the St. Lawrence and up as far as Montreal. Frobisher, Davis and Baffin sought for a passage farther north, but found only rocky shores and ice-choked seas. Henry Hudson pushed up the Hudson River and deep into Hudson Bay, but gave up his life in vain. It was not granted to those men to know that they had opened up great channels of trade and colonization; they ended their lives believing only that they had failed in their chosen task of finding the passage to China.

William Baffin, the last of these early discoverers, died in 1622, and for the next two hunred years no serious attempt was made to sail around the north end of Canada. It was plain that if there was a Northwest Passage, it was too difficult and dangerous for profitable commerce. So discovery in the far north was neglected. The fur traders, Samuel Hearne and Alexander Mackenzie, just reached the shore of the Arctic at the mouths of the Coppermine and Mackenzie Rivers respectively; for the rest, as late as 1819, all the way from the east of Baffin Land to the west of Alaska, nothing was known of the Arctic coast of North America, or of the islands that lay beyond it.

In the meantime people's minds were being broadened and their interests quickened by what we call the Scientific Revolution.

The explorers of the sixteenth century had gone abroad in search of profit and adventure. The men of the nineteenth century sought out new lands to study their plants, animals, and geological structure; they measured winds, tides, and fields of magnetism. John Barrow, Secretary to the British Admiralty, was much interested in these problems, and to him belongs the credit for the renewal of discovery in the Canadian Arctic. At his suggestion, in 1819, Lieutenant Edward Parry was given the ships *Hecla* and *Griper* with orders to seek an ocean passage to the north of the American continent, and, with the aid of a small staff of "naturalists", to add what he could to scientific knowledge.

Parry found his way up Baffin Bay, through Lancaster Sound into the maze of islands that lay beyond; and in the most successful voyage ever made by sailing ships in those waters, he sailed around surf-beaten rocks and through broken ice-fields as far as Melville Island. There he spent the winter of 1819–20 at Winter Harbour, and carved the names of his vessels on Parry's Monument, a huge sandstone rock that stood on the beach.

In the next summer, sailing west to Cape Hay, he found himself on the margin of the frozen expanse of the Beaufort Sea, whose huge ice floes, drifting east, jammed up the channel of Melville Sound and blocked his further advance. To the southwest across Melville Sound he dimly made out a "loom of land" to which he gave the name of Banks Land. The names and location of these features should be kept in mind, for they had important bearing on the movements of the *Investigator* thirty years later.

Subsequent voyages by Parry and by the Rosses—John and James—were less successful, though they furnished some knowledge of the west shore of Regent's Inlet, Boothia Isthmus, and King William Island, and also fixed the position of the North Magnetic Pole.

While Parry and the Rosses were at work among the islands, land-based expeditions were busy a little to the south along the continental shore. In 1819, the year of Parry's first voyage, Lieutenant John Franklin was sent overland through Canada to chart its Arctic coast by canoe. In one of the epic journeys of discovery, he tramped through the Canadian Northland in the dead of winter, descended the Coppermine by canoe and mapped hundreds of miles of shore-line to the east of its mouth; but, caught by the early approach of winter, he barely struggled back to the friendly Indians of the Slave Lake area with the loss of ten of the nineteen men who accompanied him.

The lessons taught by this partial and costly success were quickly learned; in later boat journeys, by Franklin and his friend Dr. John Richardson (1825–27), and by the fur traders Dease and Simpson (1836–39), the continental shore was mapped all the way from Alaska east to the mouth of the Great Fish (Back's) River. In twenty years these men had achieved a vast amount of discovery. The Canadian north shore, quite unknown before, was almost completely charted, and the map of the islands beyond had come to resemble a jig-saw puzzle that is unfinished but beginning to show a recognizable pattern.

In 1845 the Admiralty equipped two ships to find an ocean link connecting the discoveries of Parry among the islands with those of Franklin and Simpson on the mainland, and so complete the Northwest Passage. Sir John Franklin, now nearly sixty years old, pleaded hard to be given the command. "If you don't send him," said Parry to one of the Lords of the Admiralty, "he will die of disappointment." In July of 1845 Franklin's two ships, the *Erebus* and the *Terror,* disappeared into the ice fields of Baffin Bay, and neither they nor any of the hundred and thirty who manned them were ever seen again.

In 1848, as Franklin was still unreported, Sir James Ross was sent with the ships *Enterprise* and *Investigator* to bring him aid. Ross made his way through Lancaster Sound, but neither in that nor in the next year did the state of the ice permit him to get past Somerset Island. His sledge parties searched a great part of the shores of the island without finding the least trace of the lost ships, and in the autumn of 1849 he returned to England to report his ill success. Two of the officers who served on this cruise were an elderly Irish lieutenant, Robert McClure, and his younger compatriot, Leopold McClintock.

It was now certain that Franklin's ships had been either wrecked or permanently trapped in the ice, and that his crews were stranded somewhere, perishing from cold and hunger. But where? They might be anywhere from Canada's north shore to the Pole. It was determined to search this vast area from both east and west. So, while Captain Horatio Austin was appointed to take a squadron in again by Lancaster Sound, the *Enterprise* and *Investigator* were refitted to sail into the western Arctic by way of Cape Horn, the Pacific Ocean, and Bering Strait.

They were deeply laden with three years' supplies, their hulls braced within and reinforced without to withstand better the blows and pressure of the ice. As this made them very slow sailing, they were hurried off in January 1850 to give them a better chance of covering the many thousands of miles that lay between them and their destination, before the autumn freeze-up. In command of the expedition was Captain Richard Collinson of the *Enterprise,* seconded by Robert McClure (promoted commander) in the *Investigator.*

To make their search as thorough as possible, both officers were instructed to call at Eskimo settlements in North Alaska for news of the castaways; and on learning that the Moravian Church had missions to the Eskimos in both Greenland and Labrador, the Admiralty requested it to furnish them with an interpreter. The leaders of the order recommended John A. Miertsching, a pious brother, who had spent some years at a Labrador mission, and was then on furlough in Germany. Miertsching gladly accepted the post, hurried to England, and, as we have seen, arrived at Plymouth just in time to tumble on board the *Investigator* after she had her anchor up. And so, at a time when he had expected to be relaxing with his widowed mother in Saxony, the young German found himself tossing on the Atlantic in the wildest and stormiest January that his shipmates could remember.

Chapter two

A man of daring and resource

THE TWO SHIPS—not, as we have mentioned, warships built for speed and handiness, but cargo vessels chosen because they could carry supplies for a cruise of several years' duration—were poor sailers. The *Investigator* proved to be the poorer of the two; and in consequence of carrying too much sail in an effort to keep up with her consort, she snapped her foretopmast in the gale and had to heave to for repairs.

While she was thus engaged the *Enterprise* came alongside, and Collinson sent word aboard that sailing in company in that abominable weather was causing needless trouble and strain to both crews: they would proceed independently and rendezvous at Cape Lisburne on the Alaskan coast. From there they would go into the Arctic together in obedience to the orders that required them on no account to separate in the ice.

The *Enterprise* then set sail and disappeared into the storm, leaving her consort to complete her repairs and follow as best she could. McClure, a shy and reserved man, gave no hint of what he thought; but Miertsching heard other officers grumbling that Collinson wished to leave them behind, and take to himself and his own ship the credit for whatever the expedition might accomplish.

Left to herself, the stout *Investigator* ploughed steadily southward through the warm waters and sunny weather of the tropics into the south latitudes, and towards Cape Horn and the stormiest waters in the world. There terrible gales struck the ship head on. A sailing ship could work its way against a moderate breeze ("beat to windward") by tacking; but in a storm so strong that she could carry little or no sail, she had no chance. The *Investigator* was driven back on her course over a hundred miles—a maddening experience to her crew, whose comrade ship was already ahead of them, and who knew that unless they reached Bering Strait before autumn, a whole season would be wasted.

At last the storm abated, and with milder and more favourable breezes they headed south again. Three months after quitting Plymouth, they made out through fog and rain the white cliffs of Cape Virgins. This headland marked the east entrance of Magellan Strait, a narrow, crooked channel, but often preferred by captains who feared the stormy passage around Cape Horn.

As they entered the strait they sighted a steamboat coming out of a bay, and were overjoyed when she signalled that she was H.M.S. *Gorgon,* and had come to give them a tow. Her captain reported that he had met the *Enterprise,* but had been ordered by Collinson to wait and give the slower *Investigator* a lift. Evidently the officers of the latter had been unjust to their senior commander. The *Gorgon* was a small and feeble boat according to our notions, but she proved the value of steam power. In a few days she hauled the heavy and clumsy freighter through the tidal currents of a twisting, rocky channel that would have cost her own crew many weeks of toil and danger to get through.

All were impressed by the wild and rugged beauty of the scenery on both sides of the strait. The island of Terra del Fuego, which formed its southern side, had been visited a few years before by the great biologist, Charles Darwin, who had there made some of the observations that were later to make him famous. The ship's surgeon, Dr. Alexander Armstrong, himself a keen scientist, was very anxious to land and make a study of the island's plant and animal life; but of course the time could not be spared.

As they were nearing the western outlet of the strait they came up with the *Enterprise* toiling ahead under sail. The stout little *Gorgon* promptly hitched herself to both vessels, and in smooth water still made good time; but on emerging from the narrow channel and meeting the mountainous rollers of the Pacific she broke her tow, and after one or two ineffectual attempts to recover it, gave up and steamed back into the calmer waters of the strait. About the same time the *Enterprise* was lost sight of in thick weather, and the *Investigator* never saw her again.

Fairly out in the Pacific, the ship met furious gales, at first from the north, that drove her off course again and south to the latitude of Cape Horn. Later they veered to the west, and the ship was able to set a northerly course up the South American coast with the wind on her beam. The storms continued without interruption for five weeks, and the gallant little ship laboured on, burrowing deep through the green rollers and wallowing in the trough of the sea. As the waves were continually washing over the deck, the hatches were battened down and all skylights closed and covered.

Poor Miertsching, who was accustomed to the crisp, dry air of Labrador, formed a very unfavourable idea of the life of a sailor. The ship's interior, where sixty-six men were housed, was dark and foul from lack of ventilation; whenever a hatch was opened the water came pouring in, and cascaded back and forth as the ship pitched and rolled, while the entire hull creaked and groaned with the strain. There was no escape from these trials, as the sick bay was as wet, leaky and uncomfortable as the rest of the ship.

Finally the storm subsided and the weather grew warm as they neared the tropics. Hatches were opened to air the lower deck, and clothes were hung on the rigging to dry. With favourable winds the old ship was making a hundred miles a day, and once sailed a hundred and eighty-six miles in twenty-four hours—a record for the sluggish *Investigator*.

On June 25th the top of a snow-covered mountain appeared over the rim of the horizon, and was joyfully hailed as the Mona Roa of Hawaii. This and the island of Maui were soon passed, and the ship hove to off Honolulu harbour. While waiting for a pilot the officers eagerly scanned the port with telescopes, hoping to make out the *Enterprise,* but in vain; and when the pilot came aboard, he confirmed their fears—she was no longer there. Collinson had arrived on the 25th, taken on supplies, and sailed the day before the *Investigator* hove in sight. He left written instructions for McClure, which strengthened the officer's fears that, despite orders, the *Investigator* might be left behind.

The ship had taken five months and eleven days from Plymouth to Honolulu—a journey that by modern air transport might be measured in hours.

The Hawaiian Islands were not then a territory of the United States, but a sovereign state under the rule of a native prince with European advisers. But Honolulu was already a thriving seaport, visited by the ships of many nations. The men of H.M.S. *Swift,* which was anchored there, volunteered to attend to the lading of the *Investigator,* and so freed her crew for the last shore leave they were to enjoy for several years to come.

Collinson's orders gave McClure the impression that if the *Investigator* was not on hand at Cape Lisburne, he would take the permanent look-out ship *Plover* with him into the ice, and leave the *Investigator* in its place in Kotzebue Sound on the west shore of Alaska. McClure and his men were much upset at the prospect of being robbed of the honourable service assigned them, and not least of all Miertsching, who was adventurous as he was pious, and had not given up his furlough and endured the discomforts of a long sea voyage to be stranded in an Alaskan bay and suffer the hardships of a high latitude without the glory of a voyage into the deep Arctic.

But McClure was a man of daring and resource. To the north, between him and Bering Strait, lay the Aleutian chain, an extended maze of island and shoal, often shrouded in fog. Collinson intended to avoid this dangerous obstacle by setting a course to the north-west around its western end, and from there north-east to Bering Strait—a safe but long and tiresome route. McClure made up his mind to gamble on the short cut.

On quitting Honolulu and rounding the island of Oahu, he set a northerly course straight for the islands. As they drew near to this dangerous region the fog grew so thick that from time to time they would hear a thump aloft as some sea-bird flew blindly into the rigging.

In these unknown waters reefs and sand-bars were a terrible danger. Had he not been in such haste McClure would have hove to and waited until he could see where he was going. As it was he sent a man to the masthead with orders that if he could not see he was to *listen* for the roar of the surf breaking on rocks, and stationed another man in the bows with the lead (a lead weight with a length of rope attached) to sound the depth of the sea and give warning when it grew too shallow for safety. With this lead continually going, McClure groped his way through the treacherous shallows of the island chain. He was aided by a momentary lift in the fog that revealed "a bluff point, with a detached rock lying off it . . . and this was all they saw of the Aleutian chain". It was enough to satisfy them that they were on course and to renew their hope and confidence. They were soon clear of the Aleutians and steered for the Diomede Islands and the entrance to Bering Strait.

The channel between the Diomede Islands, which now separates the territories of the United States from those of the Soviet Republic, was the most dangerous piece of navigation of the whole voyage. Fog reduced visibility to four hundred yards, and a fair wind was carrying them too rapidly through narrows where the tide ran with the force of a cataract. "The noise was so great that you could not hear what was said without great vocal exertion; the sea was breaking into the channels, and the deep sea lead showed that the ship was sweeping over twenty-two fathoms' water only".

After some anxious hours soundings began to grow deeper, the deadly tide ripple died away as the channel grew broader, and the *Investigator* had won through, many days ahead of the faster-sailing *Enterprise*. As they were now in the Arctic Circle, winter clothing was issued to the men.

Two other rescue ships were then cruising in Bering Strait, the *Plover* and the *Herald*. The *Plover* was stationed permanently off Alaska during the years of the Franklin search, to gather news from the Eskimos and to send boats into the Arctic to scout during the summer months. The *Herald* came up annually to bring her supplies. Neither ship was fitted for close encounter with the ice.

The *Investigator* passed the *Plover* and exchanged greetings with her; and off Cape Lisburne, the rendezvous appointed by Collinson, she met Captain Kellett in the *Herald*. Both ships hove to, and McClure with some of his officers went aboard and made the acquaintance not of Kellett only, but also of a young mate (sub-lieutenant), Bedford Pim, whom he was to meet again under very different circumstances. Miertsching was delighted to meet a fellow-German, Berthold Seeman, the *Herald's* naturalist.

An eager discussion arose between the two captains. McClure, by a lucky accident, found himself for the moment his own master; for Collinson, who had never dreamed that the *Investigator* would beat him in the race to Cape Lisburne, had neglected to tell his junior officer what he ought to do if that happened. McClure, finding himself at liberty to use his own judgment, resolved to sail on alone. Collinson, he said, might at the last moment have chosen the same short cut as himself; in the fog he could have passed the straits unobserved by the *Plover* or the *Herald,* and so might still be ahead of him. Kellett, convinced that the prudent Collinson would have taken the safe route around the islands, urged McClure to wait. The latter returned to his ship and gave orders to set sail and proceed.

As the *Investigator* gathered way her officers noticed a cluster of flags slowly mounting to the *Herald's* peak, and they studied them with anxiety. Captain Kellett outranked Commander McClure, and could, if he chose, *order* him to stay. But the signal flags merely spelt out the polite suggestion: "Had you not better wait forty-eight hours?" McClure signalled back that it was his duty to go on. The fast-sailing *Herald* ran up alongside, and through the megaphone Kellett hailed a request that the signal might be repeated—a hint that he understood it all right, but was far from approving it. The stubborn McClure ordered the signal repeated.

Watching from the quarter-deck of the *Herald,* Kellett shrugged his shoulders. Collinson was his intimate friend, but McClure was a brother-Irishman, and after all it was Collinson's fault for framing his orders so carelessly. So he hoisted the "Good luck" signal and sheered off, leaving the *Investigator* to pursue her lonely and dangerous course.

With all the Canadian Arctic to choose from, McClure had already determined where to direct his search. The British discoverers (Franklin among them) who had mapped the north shore of Alaska knew nothing whatever of the waters that lay beyond it. But a thousand miles to the north-east of Cape Lisburne, on the far side of the great unknown, lay Parry's Melville Island and Winter Harbour, and also the faint "loom of land" that he had called Banks Land.

It was for this unknown country that McClure resolved to steer, for two reasons. First, he thought that Franklin might have followed in Parry's track, and have been imprisoned in the great ice-floes from which Parry had barely escaped. (He did not suspect that this very accident was to happen to himself.) Second, if he could reach from the west the land that Parry had sighted from the east, the Northwest Passage from ocean to ocean was discovered, and the glory belonged to him and his ship alone.

Chapter three

The dwellers on the lonely shore

McCLURE SOON found that he could not set a course straight for Banks Land. As he steered north-east from Cape Lisburne, the well-known "ice-blink" appeared in the sky, and soon he saw the flash of surf breaking on a continuous barrier of ice that lay off shore and fenced him in to the Alaskan coast. So he began to pick his way east, with the ice on his left hand, and on his right a gently sloping beach that pushed out seawards in ribs of submerged sand-bars—a nightmare for the navigator, especially when he had no detailed charts to warn him where danger lay. The twenty-four-hour daylight of the Arctic Circle did something to lessen the risk.

Once they saw a herd of walrus sunning themselves on the ice with their young. Some ardent sportsmen on board loaded one of the ship's guns to fire among them, but this cruel and useless act was promptly forbidden by the captain. Seeing a gap in the ice-field, he steered into it; but finding that the avenue narrowed, and fearing that the ship might become permanently stuck—"beset" as it was called—he put about and continued to feel his way along the shore.

They were now approaching the cape of Point Barrow, the northernmost point of the Alaskan shore; and all on board were impatient to arrive, for the crew of the *Plover* had declared that they could not get past—the ice lay so close to the cape that nothing larger than a boat could squeeze by. Luck, however, was with the *Investigator*. As she approached the cape it was seen that southerly winds had driven the ice off shore, and she found nothing in her way except loose fragments, which she bumped and pushed aside without suffering any damage. When the wind failed at a critical moment, the crew hoisted out the boats and towed her in triumph into the open expanse of water on the east side of the cape. Miertsching, who was as much at home with Eskimos as with Europeans, now enjoyed the daily prospect of meeting the people among whom he had lived for so long.

The Eskimos of North America and Greenland then lived a life that was extraordinary according to our notions. They had no metals, and no wood except what was washed down by the rivers of America and Siberia to the sea, and cast ashore as drift-wood. Out of wood and bone they fashioned weapons with which they hunted the seal, the walrus, and the caribou. They made boats by drawing hides over a framework of wood, and lived in huts built of stone, or, in the winter, of snow. They were a happy, good-natured, contented folk, who seldom caused trouble to the explorers, and often showed them voluntary kindness.

A day or two after passing Point Barrow, Miertsching was called from his bed at 3 A.M. Eskimos had been seen on shore. He mounted to the deck in the chill of the early morning air, and found the boat already lowered, with the captain and the sailing-master, Mr. Court, in it. As they neared the beach Miertsching was pleased to see that in appearance and dress the natives closely resembled the Eskimos of Labrador; and on landing he found that their language was similar to that of the people among whom he had worked before. They received him with kindness, and readily answered his questions, but could give no information about the lost ships.

While Miertsching was making these enquiries, his comrades were doing what they could to show friendship to a people whose language they did not understand. "While Captain McClure was giving out some tobacco as a present, he felt a hand in his trousers pocket, and on looking down found a native actually, while receiving a gift with one hand, picking his pocket with the other. Yet when detected, the fellow laughed so good-humouredly, and all his compatriots seemed to enjoy the joke so amazingly, that even the aggrieved parties joined in the merriment."

It would certainly have been wrong and foolish for the visitors to quarrel with these Alaskan folk, when their own countrymen might be wandering thereabouts, dependent on their kindness. Through Miertsching, McClure told the natives that he was looking for a lost brother and his companions; the Eskimos replied with warmth and sincerity that if they met the castaways they would show them kindness and "give them deer's flesh". They boarded their kayaks and accompanied the boat to the ship, where they were given a hospitable reception and sent away with gifts.

Further along the coast they met another group of natives who had never seen white men. These, though not hostile, were frightened and uneasy: it was some time before Miertsching could win their confidence and get them to talk. They kept their eyes fixed on the *Investigator*, lying offshore, and at every movement of the vessel made as though they would run away.

Miertsching, always deeply interested in their religious beliefs, found that they believed in a Good and a Bad Spirit, and that a man fared well or ill in the after life according to his behaviour in this. When the Eskimos at last overcame their fears and paddled off to the ship, it was found that in spite of what Miertsching calls their "informed consciences", they were not entirely to be trusted. Several small articles were missing, and one stout fellow was caught trying to make off with an ice-anchor that weighed fifty-six pounds.

A few days later they arrived off the mouth of the Mackenzie, where the silt washed down by the river made the waters of its estuary shallow and particularly dangerous. In spite of all precautions, the ship struck on a shoal. As soundings showed that she was stuck on the very top of the sand-bar, McClure first tried to force her over, but this only fixed her more firmly. Sails were taken in and anchors run out from the stern to heave her off with the capstan. She refused to budge.

The boats were next hoisted out and loaded with all the provisions and other cargo they could carry, in order to lighten the ship; and when the men again put their weight to the capstan bars, they were cheered by a cry from the leadsman that she was beginning to give. With gathering momentum she slid off the shoal, and was again afloat. Unluckily the sea was growing rough, and one boat capsized with the loss of nearly two tons of meat— a grievous misfortune, as it later proved, but at the time the explorers were probably too much relieved at their escape from shipwreck to care.

In that maze of shoals McClure no longer dared to manoeuvre the ship under sail; he ordered the boats to take her in tow and, after two days of sounding and weaving about, was again in the clear. To avoid another such accident he set a course north into the ice, but got into trouble there also, and slanted his course back to the American shore. His detour was not altogether a wasted effort; he had circled around the greater part of the shallows of the Mackenzie estuary.

A little to the east, at Point Warren, an Eskimo encampment was seen on shore four miles away. The water was too shallow for the ship to venture closer in, so the Captain, with Dr. Armstrong and Miertsching, at once took to the boat. It was now late August, the sky was dull, and the wind, blowing from the north off the ice, made it bitterly cold. The boat grounded fifty yards from the beach, and all were thoroughly drenched in wading ashore.

The natives were gathered a little distance away, brandishing their weapsons in a very threatening manner. To show fear or hestitation was to invite attack, so McClure, Armstrong and the seamen advanced slowly, while Miertsching paused to slip into his Eskimo dress. When he came up and spoke to the natives in their own tongue they became less hostile in tone, but would admit of no friendly relations unless the white men would carry away their firearms and put them in the boat. McClure ordered this to be done, and submitted himself and his men unarmed to the natives. By this courageous act of trustfulness he at once won their friendship and confidence.

Having first learned that the Eskimos knew nothing of Franklin and his men, Miertsching introduced McClure to them as a great chief, and Armstrong as a medicine chief. Both were welcomed with great respect, and the doctor was invited to examine a young man, the son of the native chief, who had broken his ankle while hunting. Armstrong tells us that he was greatly touched by the care and gentleness with which the boy's mother removed his moccasin and laid bare the injured limb. It was much mortified, and the doctor asked permission to take the boy to the ship and perform an amputation. After some hesitation the parents declined to let him out of their hands.

"The unhappy young man," says Miertsching, "had probably but a few weeks to live. I now remembered a deplorable custom of the Eskimos, when they move from one district to another. If they have on their hands an invalid who is difficult to carry, they leave him in some place secure from wild beasts, with a little food, and from that moment think of him no more." Armstrong was much impressed with the handsome features of the young man and with his patient endurance of his coming fate.

Seeing that the hospitable natives had built a blazing fire of driftwood, Armstrong left his patient and walked over to warm and dry himself. There he noticed that the old chief, who stood near him, wore in his ear a button of European manufacture. At the doctor's request Miertsching asked him how he obtained it, and the old man answered with the greatest frankness. It was part of the clothing of a white man who had come to their encampment and, having made himself disagreeable, had been killed not many yards from where they stood. He pointed to a grave, which, after some study, Miertsching declared not to be that of an Eskimo.

This story puzzled the white men. No discovery expedition had lost a man in that manner, and the nearest trading post was far away. The Eskimos always had trouble in expressing the duration of time, and Miertsching confessed that he could not tell how remote the incident was, though it had probably happened too long ago to relate to the Franklin expedition. The natives had nothing more to tell, and their visitors departed with the mystery unsolved.

Still coasting to the east along the inner edge of the ice-pack, they sighted a group of tents and stone huts near Cape Bathurst, and again the boat was sent away. This time Miertsching took the precaution of putting on his Eskimo clothing before leaving the ship. The Eskimos ran down to the beach waving their bows and lances in a threatening manner, but on seeing Miertsching's dress, and hearing him speak, they at once became friendly. "Soon they brought their wives and children, and, to prove their trust in us, put their infant babes in our arms."

They were much amused at seeing one of the ship's officers lose his sea boots in the mud while wading ashore; when he was seen to take a long pull at a pocket flask they cried out in horror that it was poison, the white man's fire-water. Miertsching gravely explained that it was taken as medicine to ward off a cold, whereupon an Eskimo girl complained of a pain and begged for a dram—which she found not at all to her taste.

As soon as the zealous missionary had made sure that they knew nothing of the lost ships, he began to question them about their religion and to tell them of his own.

> I doubt if their theory of the stars would be found among any other people. The sun, they say, quits for a time his great blue mansion (referring to the short summer in the polar regions); he then returns and watches what is happening on earth through a multitude of little holes . . . we call stars. After death those who on earth "have fed the widows and orphans" go to a country where the Good Spirit prevents the game from running away. Seal and caribou are there without number. In that country there are no tempests and no ice, but a mild and even warmth produced by a sun which never sets.
>
> As they were about to tell me what happens in the country governed by the Evil Spirit, to which the wicked go, I heard the captain calling me. At once the old chief, Kenalualik, entreated me to stay and tell them of many things which they wished to know.

"I cannot: I must accompany these men who are searching for friends lost in the ice-fields." But Kenalualik would not let me go; he held me by the arm, offering me a tent to live in, his daughter for a wife, and a sledge fully equipped with which to rejoin the ship when the sea froze over. I did not know how to refuse, especially when I would so gladly have remained among these poor folk to tell them the Gospel. At last the captain himself came to look for me.

The boat's crew returned to the ship accompanied by their new-found friends in a convoy of fifteen kayaks. There Miertsching assisted in a distribution of gifts, and "I could not help giving more than his fair share of my old friend Kenalualik". (There were more ways than one of obtaining an extra handout.)

When the crowd of kayaks was around the ship a sailor noticed on board an Eskimo clothed in rags and trembling with the cold. Moved with pity the brave fellow clothed him in a good pair of trousers. Half an hour later the same unfortunate, again in rags, appeared on another part of the deck. The captain observed him, and, stirred with compassion in his turn, commanded his servant to give him some warm clothing. Puffed up with this success the Eskimo wished to try his luck again, but this time he was caught.

The men of the *Investigator* continued their voyage to the east with a growing feeling of impatience and discouragement. They had been in the Arctic for over a month, in the most difficult sort of navigation, and all their toil and anxiety had gone for nothing. They had found no traces of the ships for which they sought; nor were they making geographical discoveries, for they were on the coast which Franklin himself had mapped on an earlier expedition; and day after day their hopes were mocked by the sight of the endless ice barrier that shut them off from the islands to the north. They were almost due south of Banks Land, and would soon be moving beyond and away from it. On rounding Cape Bathurst they found the coast trending to the south-east, and the ice following it to force them further from their objective, and under the four-hundred-foot cliffs of Franklin Bay.

Heavy columns of smoke were seen rising along the shore. Miertsching declared that no Eskimos would burn fuel in that extravagant manner, and it was suggested that what they saw was the signal fires of the lost crews. Dr. Armstrong and Miertsching landed and scrambled up the loose slope of a recent landslide to learn the truth. They found a number of smoking cones, caused, Armstrong said, by lime, sulphur, and other chemicals burning underground. Miertsching brought back to the ship a few cinders, which burnt his pocket handkerchief and his mahogany desk, and so had to be kept in a tumbler.

That day was the turning-point in the cruise. If the *Investigator* had remained on that coast a few days longer, she would have been frozen in for the winter, and might never have achieved an important success. But that night, September 5th, strong winds from the south-west drove back the ice and allowed McClure at last to set the northerly course that he had twice before attempted in vain. Before noon of the 6th land was reported to the north-east, and a massive peak of limestone was seen rising higher and higher above the sea as the ship drew nearer. It proved to be a great cliff, falling steeply into the sea, and backed by hills that were even higher. McClure drew under it, as close inshore as he dared, and hoisted out the boats to give as many men as possible the pride of treading on "new land". He named his discovery Baring Land, though he suspected that it was the south end of Parry's Banks Land. The cape first sighted was called Nelson Head.

Re-embarking, the adventurous crew began to coast along the rocky shore to the east and north, and soon saw on the horizon ahead a dark line, which, as they neared it, took the shape of more new land, separated from Baring Land by a deep bay with no visible bottom, which might prove to be a strait leading to open waters beyond. Should they enter it, and again undergo the strain of weaving through a narrow channel, plus the risk of being locked by ice in a closed basin? McClure obtained a careful fix of his position before making up his mind.

Chapter four

Deep in the ice

Y OU MAY wonder how a sailor knows where he is, out in mid-ocean, far from any landmark. He fixes his position by determining how far north or south he is of the equator, (his latitude) and how far east or west of the north-south meridian passing through Greenwich, England (his longitude). The altitude of the sun, measured by sextant, gives him his latitude. This method was understood by the ancient Greeks; but until recently no satisfactory way of measuring longitude had been known.

It increases our admiration for the Portuguese and Spanish sailors, who made such wonderful voyages in the Pacific and Indian Oceans, when the navies of England, France and Holland were in their infancy, when we learn that they had to judge their longitude by "dead reckoning", by estimating how far they had travelled east or west from some known point; and they could be, and sometimes were, hundreds of miles off in their reckoning.

But in McClure's time there was no more of this dangerous guesswork. His ship carried a chronometer, a very accurate kind of clock, which was always kept on Greenwich time. Consulting this, the captain found that when the sun was at its zenith off Nelson Head it was 8 P.M. at Greenwich. The sun travels fifteen degrees in an hour, so his longitude was 120 degrees west. His latitude was found to be between 71 and 72 north.

Parry's "farthest" on his great voyage in from the east had been about 74 north and 113 west, still a long way from where the *Investigator* lay. But Parry had *seen* many miles further over the frozen sea of Melville Sound, and McClure reckoned that if he could find water for a little over a hundred miles, he would reach Melville Sound, tie up his voyage from the Pacific with

Parry's from the Atlantic, and complete the Northwest Passage, which for three hundred years had been sought in vain. If the risk was great, so was the prize. McClure steered in between the two lands.

And so the little ship sailed into the unknown, with great cliffs on the right hand and on the left. Sheltered from the ocean swell, the waters were calm, and would, says Armstrong, have resembled a lake in the Scottish Highlands, but for the stupendous ice barrier that lay in an unbroken line along the precipitous shore. In places the sea shallowed to thirty-six feet, and they were always on the alert for shoals. For a time the waters appeared to be narrowing to a dead end, but on rounding a cape they saw with joy the channel broadening out again, its surface broken by two rocky islets, the Princess Royal Islands. These they passed, but beyond them met their old enemy, huge masses of ice drifting down on them in ever increasing density.

It was the luck of the *Investigator,* that year and the next, to miss success by a hair's breadth. She was, it was reckoned, only thirty miles from Melville Sound when the channel became wholly blocked by ice driving down before a gale. To avoid being pushed ashore, McClure anchored his ship to a huge floe, and was swept back with it, past the Princess Royal Islands and many miles to the south. Then the wind changed and carried them forward again, until through the driving snow they made out the island looming ahead and almost overhanging them.

But McClure had chosen wisely. The floe to which he was anchored drew much more water than the ship; it caught on the sea-bottom, and began to pivot. The crew, gazing fascinated at the rocks on which they were driving, saw them beginning to recede, and realized that the ice sheet to which they were fixed was turning and swinging them away from the land. Then, as the wind subsided, all motion died away, and the ship began to freeze in. It was late September, and the Arctic winter was upon them.

But another trial awaited them. A day or two later, before the floating masses around had become solidly fixed in a bed of "young ice", another gale came roaring down the strait from the north. The ice stirred and heaved until the ship's timbers creaked and groaned with the pressure. Preparations were made to abandon ship; provisions were stacked on deck; and each man was ordered to make ready a bundle of necessaries to carry with him if the worst happened and he had to jump on the ice.

In times of perplexity and danger it used to be, and perhaps still is, the practice of some good people to open their Bibles at random and, with eyes closed, to put the finger on a text, which was accepted as God's answer to the problem that troubled them. Miertsching, who was thoroughly frightened, did this, and received the rather threatening response: "Be ye therefore ready, for ye know neither the day nor the hour when the Son of Man cometh." So he lay down fully dressed and expecting the worst.

For the early part of the night there was a lull; then an increasing gale again drove the ice down the strait. Old floes were set in motion, telescoping the young ice between them, and when their course was checked by the islands in mid-channel, they jammed and began to pile up in the most incredible manner. "Masses of ice, four times the size of the ship, would be heaped up one on the other by the force of the hurricane, and would collapse with an uproar that was truly appalling."

Caught in the pressure, the ship groaned like a tortured animal; tar was squeezed from her seams in strips; her frame was wrenched until the walls of cabins split, and their doors would neither open nor close. The churning masses on her weather side piled up to the height of her foreyard, and, strong as she was, she must have crumpled, had not a projecting tongue of ice been forced under her keel, and lifting her up bodily, flung her on her broadside with a crazy tilt against the floe to which she was still anchored.

There she lay for some hours, until the gale died down, the pressure slackened, and the crowded ice masses began to sag away to the north. The ship slowly righted and eased back into the opening from which she had been sprung. All hands were ordered to remain on deck while the captain and the carpenter went below to measure the damage. To the general relief, they reported no leaks.

24

A grim but necessary ceremony followed. When the d
was at its height, some panic-stricken sailors had "forced the
of the locker where the liquor was stored, in order to escaj
drunkenness from the agonies of death." The captain now c
the crew together, and, baring his head, read the part ot
Regulations that related to the disciplinary powers of a comm
ing officer. He then passed sentence on the offenders, and
next day they were bound to the rigging and flogged. It
hard measure for the poor, fear-crazed wretches; but the terrify
danger that afforded some excuse for the offence *morally,* d
heightened their misconduct from the standpoint of naval di
pline and the safety of the ship.

In a few days the *Investigator* was frozen in solidly. Just
the west of where she lay were the Princess Royal Islands, a
beyond them rose the cliffs of Baring (or Banks) Land. On t
other side of the strait to the east lay the country that McClu
had named Prince Albert, but which was later found to be pa
of Victoria Island. As the ship was not likely to move for te
months, her topmasts were taken down and stowed; and a grea
canvas housing was drawn over the upper deck to give the crev
shelter from the wind while exercising.

Though the size and quantity of the masses of ice that had
come pouring down from the north and had all but wrecked the
ship convinced her officers that it was no bay they had entered,
but a through channel opening out into a much larger body of
water beyond, McClure was not satisfied. He must see it before
he would believe it. He hoped that the towering cliffs of Prince
Albert Land would give a clear view of what lay to the north;
so, a few days after the storm, when he thought that all the water
lanes would be securely frozen over, he set out for the land, which
lay some five miles away. He chose as his companions his second
lieutenant, Mr. Cresswell; Dr. Armstrong, Miertsching, and four
seamen.

Close under the cliffs they came upon a feature of the sea-ice
that was new to them, but was to become very familiar to later
travellers in the Arctic. This was the "tide-crack". In the bitter

cold of the North the shallow water in shore freezes to the sea bottom, and becomes a solid, immovable border of shore ice, while farther out the surface of the frozen sea rises and sinks with the tide. Thus it tends to break away from the fast shore ice and form a tide-crack, sometimes closed, but sometimes open to a considerable width. Our travellers found it closed,—in fact the sea ice had been driven in shore with such force as to grind away part of the solid ice foot and heave it up into a ridge of rubble several feet high. The explorers vaulted over this and continued their journey without giving it another thought. They were to pay more attention to the tide-crack on their way back to the ship.

They reached land and climbed up a low, sandy ridge. There the sailors remained to build a cairn of stones as a memorial of their visit. The officers, in the meantime, toiled up a snow-covered slope to the top of a mountain fourteen hundred feet high. From that point they had a magnificent view of the frozen strait they had just quitted—all under a thick blanket of snow, here level and glaring bright in the sun, there thrown up into variously shaped mounds by the hummocks and ridges of the ice. In the background was the shore of Baring Land; nearer, under the bare and shadowed cliffs of one of the Princess Royal Islands, lay the dismasted hulk of the *Investigator,* tucked away under its canvas housing and looking very small indeed.

But it was not in that direction that the eyes of the discoverers were at first directed. They were gazing to the north. In the sunlit, frosty air they could see that the shore on which they had landed soon began to fall away to the east, while the opposite shore of Baring—or, they now plainly saw, Banks—Land continued to the north and seemed to end in a rocky cape—perhaps forty miles away. Beyond the farthest land and swelling up to the skyline lay a seemingly endless field of ice, which could only be the Melville Sound of Parry. But did their inlet extend so far in unbroken salt water? They could not tell, for a great cape jutting out from the shore of Prince Albert Land partially interrupted their view. McClure cut short an eager discussion by

declaring that he would make no claim of discovery until reaching the end of the supposed strait on foot.

Success was not yet certain, but it was more probable than ever; so they sat down cheerfully for lunch. Their teeth could make no impression on sandwiches frozen as hard as rock. So they gave up and slithered down the mountainside to rejoin the seamen, who proved to be as hungry as themselves; they had poked and hammered their frozen meat-tin into a shapeless wreck without being able to get at its contents. In the gathering darkness they descended to the beach and started out over the ice.

A black cleft appeared before them in the white of the frozen sea. The tide-crack had opened and put fifty yards of clear water between them and the ship. No piece of ice that might serve as a raft could be found, and after firing off all their ammunition in a vain effort to attract notice, the wanderers, to their no small discomposure, came across the fresh tracks of polar bear. In the meantime the first lieutenant, Mr. Haswell, had taken alarm; he was firing off guns and rockets from the ship at short intervals, and soon in the starlight the forms of searchers appeared, moving here and there among the distant hummocks. The lost men shouted with all their strength, but there was breeze enough blowing to drown their cries. Tired and hungry as they were, McClure kept them walking briskly up and down the margin of the tide-crack to keep them warm and alert. Towards midnight it fell calm and at last they made themselves heard. Out of the gloom came the voice of Mr. Court asking what was the matter?

"Never mind what's the matter—have you brought a rubber boat?"

"No."

"Then why not? You might have guessed what had happened!"

Full of apologies, the master started back to the ship, several miles away, while the travellers resigned themselves to two more hours of exposure. But luckily the true state of the case had occurred to Mr. Haswell. He had sent out another party with a Halkett rubber boat, and Mr. Court was soon back, properly equipped. Even then the work of rescue was not easy, for a strong current carried the boat far down at every crossing, and extreme care was needed to avoid puncturing her on a sharp point of ice. The travellers were, however, all ferried over in safety, and reached the ship at 2.30 A.M. with a few frost-bites, but otherwise none the worse for their adventure.

It was now mid-October. The days were growing short, and in less than a month the sun would disappear for several weeks, and there would be no day at all. Despite the increasing cold and the almost total inexperience of himself and his men in Arctic travel, the ardent McClure could not wait until spring to go up the strait and make the fact of his discovery certain. He packed a sledge with a tent and ten days' rations, chose Court and five men as his companions, and on October 21st quitted the ship for the north. He was not spared the trials and humiliations which usually fall to the lot of the beginner. After receiving an enthusiastic send-off from the entire ship's company, he broke his sledge a few hours out, and had to make an ignoble return for fresh equipment. The next day the little party was off for good.

The men whom he left behind were not idle. Miertsching, more at home in this strange environment than any other man on board, organized a hunting party to pay another visit to Prince Albert Land. The story of their adventure is best told in his own words:

29 October
  To the number of four we set out on a land excursion. Soon a pile of driftwood invited us to make a fire; we have coffee and a kettle; we sat in a circle, sipping a nectar which we found delicious because it was hot. It was then that we saw moving towards us a form which defined itself in a dark colour against the white of the snow—at first one, then two, then three. They are Eskimos! they are my friends! and there I was forming all sorts of schemes for conversing with these neighbours throughout the long winter! But whilst my imagination

was rambling and amusing itself with the details of this intercourse, the figures were coming nearer. They are not men—not bears—what are they? We hid ourselves behind a wind-tossed ridge of snow, whence we could see without being seen.

The five animals were approaching with no sign of mistrust. They were the size of an ox, bearing terrible, backward-turning horns, and clothed in hair so long that it dragged on the snow and hid their legs completely. Our guns were loaded and primed; and our hearts were beating wildly. At a distance of sixty paces the animals became aware of our presence; stopping short, they began to paw the snow and toss it with their horns, breathing noisily at the same time through their nostrils. Then the biggest advanced slowly towards us, whilst his four companions remained huddled together. He stopped at thirty paces, and began again to paw the snow and to blow. It was then that he received the first ball in his forehead. He turned about, received another bullet in his flank, and without haste placed himself beside his little flock, with his bleeding head turned towards us.

Crawling forward on our knees a few paces, we all fired and then scattered instantly. In that we were truly inspired. Growing savage the oxen rushed on us in the different directions we had taken. It was possible for us not only to avoid them but to continue our fire; the worst difficulty was, with our half-frozen fingers, to lay hold of rifle-balls. However three oxen lay on the ground when their chief wheeled round and rushed upon me. I awaited him, foot firm, rifle at the shoulder. The gun misfired, and the bullet, not properly rammed home, dropped to the ground. I tried to leap aside and fell flat on my face. The bull, more frightened than I, passed me by and kept on running. I got up, re-loaded, and followed his blood-stained footprints in the snow.

In re-reading these lines in cold blood after my return

to Europe, my impressions are quite different from those with which I wrote them. I now feel cruel; I experience a painful emotion at the idea of those harmless creatures who knew not man, and who, on first meeting him, received a bullet as a sign of man's domination. But then I did not think of that; I was a hunter to my very soul; any sort of game was welcome to the crew, who were living on salted meat. Besides the sense of danger extinguished all emotions of pity.

Finally I overtook the fugitive. One would have thought that he wished to bury himself in the snow; his legs were sunk deep in it. He was bleeding from several wounds, and one more bullet laid him low without a spark of life. At the same moment my comrades were triumphing over the last of the five, who had defended himself valiantly. Panting heavily we exchanged congratulations and blessed the Paternal Hand which had protected us. We rejoiced in the joy of our comrades, and tasted beforehand their thanks when they saw this important addition to our supplies.

The tracks of wolves and polar bears warned us of the imprudence of leaving our booty unguarded. Messrs. Sainsbury and Newton, disabled from further hunting by their frozen fingers, set out to the ship to report our success. Mr. Paine and I, while on guard, lit a fire and made coffee. Late at night a sledge arrived bearing a tent, blankets, and food. We fell asleep still talking of the success which had been the theme of our conversation all evening. In the morning a sufficient number of men and sledges came to gather up what the hunt had obtained. These animals, four cows and a bull, weighed no less (apart from the heads) than twelve hundred and ninety-six pounds. Thirteen hundredweight of fresh meat at the beginning of winter was no small blessing. The frost had almost entirely removed from the meat the smell which would otherwise have made its flavour intolerable.

Chapter five

The first winter

T HE NEXT day brought news of the absent sledge party:
31 October

This morning we saw arriving alone, in a dreadful
condition, Captain McClure, who had set out ten days
before on a sledge journey. Some miles from the ship
[on the trip back] he had left his sledge and crew behind,
and had gone forward alone, impatient, as is every bearer
of good news. He became lost in a blizzard, and wandered for twenty hours, without food or rest, because he
dared not sit down for fear of freezing to death. He had
spent all his powder in firing shots to attract the attention
of the watch. He heard all around him in the darkness
the growling of bears. [That is, in his delirium, he fancied
that he heard them.] At last the tardy Arctic dawn arrived, and revealed the *Investigator* at a distance of two
or three miles. He mustered up what strength was left
him, and fainted on reaching his cabin.

For a long time he lay there speechless. Then he told
us that the Northwest Passage, the Passage on which so
many lives and so many millions had been spent, was
discovered. He had reached it on October 26, travelling
on the ice with his sledge to the end of this strait which
we had entered. This strait opens into Barrow Strait
[more accurately, into Melville Sound, the westward ex-
pansion of Barrow Strait], which washes the shore of
Melville Island.

Thirty years before, from the heights of that island,
which he had reached from the east, Parry had made out

the eastern shore of the land which we have coasted along to the left, and to which he had given the name of Banks Land. Beyond all doubt the link between the oceans is discovered. He had named our strait Prince of Wales Strait, and had given the names of Russell and Peel to the two capes which mark its termination in Barrow Strait. Our winter quarters are at 73° 31′ N., and 114° 30′ W.

About the time that the captain recovered consciousness, Mr. Court and his party came into sight, plodding wearily towards the ship. A fatigue party that had been kept in readiness hurried to help them in. Soon they were on board and the story of their journey spread over the ship.

On the way out they had gone over to the west side of the strait and followed the shore of Baring (Banks) Land for several days. Travelling had been difficult owing to rough ice and deep snow, especially where, at high tide, water had gurgled up through cracks in the ice and turned the snow into a moist, sticky sludge. Their worst trial had been thirst, a complaint that many travellers in those regions were to make after them.

They had soon found the shore of Prince Albert Land falling away from north-east to straight east; the distant view was cut off by a cape which they named Peel. The coast of Baring Land continued in a north-easterly direction and seemed to end in a headland named Russell. McClure tried to cheer his men by assuring them that it could not be more than twelve miles away. After some hours it still seemed twelve miles away, and they realized the difficulty of judging distance in the clear air of the North.

At last they reached the cape and pitched their tent on the ice beneath it. The next day they climbed six hundred feet to its summit. They found the coast of Banks Land falling away to the north-west at right angles, and made out a ragged expanse of ocean pack stretching north and fading away in the haze. The vapour—"frost-smoke"—that rose from open water-lanes prevented them from seeing across the Sound to Melville Island, but observations made it certain that the coast on which they stood was the very "loom of land" that Parry had seen thirty years before, and that Baring and Banks were the same land. Parry's route from the east and McClure's from the west were tied together, and the Northwest Passage was discovered.

This glorious exploit, the completion after three and a half centuries of the work that John Cabot had begun, was officially recorded in a very drab entry in the ship's log:

> October 31st, the Captain returned at 8.30 A.M., and at 11.30 A.M., the remainder of the party, having, upon the 26th instant, ascertained that the waters we are now in communicate with those of Barrow Strait, the northeastern limit being in latitude 73° 31′ N., longitude 114° 39′ W., thus establishing the existence of a NORTHWEST PASSAGE between the Atlantic and Pacific Oceans.

The crew of the little ship were now faced with a task more difficult, perhaps, than the one they had just accomplished— that of fighting off the monotony of several months of semi-darkness and complete inaction. It would be April before returning daylight and moderating temperatures would permit sledge parties to set out and search for traces of Franklin; the ship herself was fixed immovably until midsummer at least. Miertsching's journal gives us an idea of how the winter was spent:

> 2 November [1850]
> The captain, restored to health, gave the crew a good dinner and a drink of grog to celebrate the discovery of the 26th.

> 11 November
> Today the sun appeared on the horizon for scarcely a minute. With what joy will we greet its return, if God preserves us for so long!

The sun, though below the horizon, gave several hours of bright twilight towards the middle of the day, and for some days the men were actively employed in this period. The *Investigator* was not deep in a sheltered harbour, but in the open sea, exposed to every wind, especially the north-easter, which blew very hard through the funnel of Prince of Wales Strait. Her crew quickly learned that a high wind was worse than the lowest of low temperatures for chilling them when indoors and freezing them when outside. So they were set to work under the direction of the ship's carpenter to cut blocks from the drifts and build a snow wall eight feet high all around the ship, as a windbreak. Mr. Ford was perhaps the first carpenter of the Royal Navy to build a snow-house, but he did his work well, and the ship, sunk within her snowy rampart, was barely visible except for her stubby lower masts, the top of her housing, and the smoke and vapour that rolled up in volumes from chimneys and air-vents.

25 November

A school is set up for the sailors, a great number of whom can neither read nor write. Certainly when as boys they went to hedge-school they did not expect that in the midst of ice, during a winter of three months, they would find one willing to instruct them. The last hour of the day is spent in music, dancing, and other recreations, in which everyone participates.

They are covering the upper deck with a sort of asphalt, which, however, we did not invent. It is composed of water, sand, and snow, which is an effective hindrance to the leakage of heat from the interior.

30 November

Two crows come daily to visit us. The cabins have a humidity, a smell of mildew, which affects our heads most painfully. We see stars continually. Today the moon is full; it does not set, but makes a complete circle in the heavens before our eyes. Our cook uses ice and snow indifferently to obtain water for his kettles. I am surprised that the ice from the ocean should be fresh; last year's ice has a slightly bitter taste; older ice gives water that is perfectly sweet.

1 December

The school for seamen is a marvellous success. They are heating cannon-balls red-hot, and are putting them in the cabins to dry the air.

11 December

A system of ventilation, invented by one of the officers, is a better cure than hot cannon-balls for the intolerable dampness. It consists of three chimneys of stout canvas which carry the air from the lower deck. While walking on the upper deck one sees this air pouring out like smoke. Each morning these pipes are cleaned, for the vapour condenses on them to the thickness of three inches.

Armstrong says of this ventilating system:

> It consisted of copper tubes from ten to sixteen inches in diameter passing through the deck, from top of which canvas funnels were attached through the housing cloth to the height of about fifteen feet. These promoted a good draught and the free escape of foul air generated below, as was evidenced by the dense volume of vapour which ever issued from their tops.

The surgeon credits the invention of this air conditioner, not to one of his brother officers, but to Lieutenant Owen Stanley of H.M.S. *Terror* during her 1836-37 cruise in Hudson Bay under Captain George Back. McClure served as mate on this voyage, and then saw the system in use which Miertsching supposes that he invented.

20 December

At thirty-five below the cold is intense. We are all shut up on the lower deck. There everyone is busy. Some are learning to spell, others are writing on slates, others already read fluently. One man is mending his clothes, others are playing cards or checkers, but all in silence so as not to disturb the students. As far as quiet goes, one must live in these regions to form an idea of the complete absence of sound. When walking abroad I can hear the ticking of my watch as soon as I stand still.

25 December

The days are beginning to grow longer. Everyone is glad. Yesterday a man made a pretence of reading print at midday.

Christmas Day was observed with a sumptuous dinner and extra grog for all hands. Miertsching was greatly shocked at what he saw:

> Christmas is being celebrated with uproarious mirth to which I am not accustomed. I do not wish to be censorious, but it wrings my heart. More than ever do I yearn for someone with whom I might talk of my Saviour. Recollections of my family, of those happy Christmases with my Eskimos in Labrador, fill my mind. I felt that I would make a foolish figure at the joyous repast, and so went out for a walk. It seemed that peace from on High descended on me from the shining stars; I shed happy tears; I blessed my Heavenly Father, blessed Him with more gratitude than ever for the gift of His Son. I would have liked to prolong my walk, but the bitter cold soon drove me back to human companionship.

But Miertsching's natural kindness was not in the least altered by what some people would think his narrowness; for he adds:

> For the rest, it would be grievous injustice if I were to speak ill of this human companionship. Here I am surrounded with friendship and respect. The prejudice conceived against me as a sour, narrow missionary has vanished. I have even some true friends whose hearts are turning towards their Saviour. The captain shows me unvarying kindness. My Heavenly Father, it is Thou who continuest to cover me with blessings.

This last paragraph is most creditable both to Miertsching and to those who voyaged with him. The young German missionary belonged to an ultra-Protestant denomination that was "other-worldly" in the strictness of its principles and in its avoidance of frivolous and noisy pleasures. Yet Miertsching, in the rough, coarse environment of the old sailing ship (and the *Investigator,* it should be noted, was not for the most part manned by regular naval ratings, but by a scratch crew, recruited for that voyage alone), was man enough not to alter his manner or disguise his prejudices, and the *Investigators* were men enough to honour him for doing so, and to welcome him, with all his difference in outlook and all his oddities, as one of themselves.

When the *Enterprise* and *Investigator* had met in the Strait of Magellan, Collinson had wished to transfer Miertsching to his own ship, where, as staff officer to the commodore, he properly belonged; but the young German had pleaded so hard against separation from the friends he had made that he was allowed to remain where he was. (Collinson, as we shall see, paid dearly for his good-natured compliance. Had Miertsching sailed with him, Collinson would in all probability have discovered the fate of Franklin, and one of the finest of all the sea-captains whom Great Britain sent into the Arctic would have won a reputation equal to his deserts.)

It must not be supposed that Miertsching was popular with everyone. Dr. Armstrong evidently disliked him, and referred to him in his journal, not by name, but contemptuously as "the interpreter". It is not difficult to see why. Though somewhat conceited and overbearing, the surgeon was probably the most intelligent and learned man on board, and it must have exasperated him to have his importance as such lessened by the talkative, informal German with his pretensions as a religious teacher, philosopher, and man of science.

On the other hand, Miertsching stood very well with the captain. The commander of a man-of-war is apt to be a lonely figure, and McClure, who found it particularly difficult to be familiar with those whom it was his duty to command, took advantage of the undefined position of the German missionary to make him a sort of confessor, and to confide in him freely. It was an odd relationship: Miertsching was a half-educated Saxon peasant, aged thirty years; McClure an Anglo-Irish aristocrat of forty-three.

31 December

The new ice—"boy ice"—thickens every day. Today it measured three and a half feet. Mammoth puddings at dinner marked the last day of the year. The sailors then produced a surprise for us—a dramatic representation of the battle of Trafalgar, which they presented with a sufficiency of intelligence and fitness.

The entry for January 6th, 1851, is a description of the daily winter routine:

I am going to relate the occupations of one of our days: it will serve as a pattern for the rest; for nothing is as monotonous as winter-quarters in the Polar Sea. At 5 A.M. the look-out man sounds the reveille. The sailors jump from their hammocks, which they roll and hang up on the wall. The first three hours of the day are devoted to those labours of exquisite cleanliness which the custom of the Navy demands. At 8 A.M. breakfast. Each man takes his place in the line at the boiler with a huge mug to receive one and a half pounds of biscuit and his cocoa. This drink, taken piping hot, affords inexpressible pleasure. The vapour of the boiler and the great number of guests usually push the thermometer up to about eight degrees above freezing-point: a short climb up a stairway, and there we are in an atmosphere of sixty degrees of frost. The contrast is somewhat harsh.

The ice has been completely levelled around the ship; there we have a little plain, convenient for walking and other exercise.

At noon sharp, dinner, composed of salt meat, dry

beans, and various preparations of flour or dried potatoes. At 1 P.M. the men return to frolic on the ice.

At 4 P.M. all return, shivering and blue with the cold. They lose no time in tasting tea and sea-biscuit. Then each man receives grog and a pipeful of tobacco.

From 6 to 8 the sailors' school. At 8.30 everyone is in bed. For those who can read, write, sketch, or knit, the time passes quickly enough. Others find it to drag.

My cabin is open without distinction of rank to everyone on board. Men come at first from sheer boredom, and repeat their visits with increasing frequency as their interest is awakened in the needs of their souls and in the infinite goodness of their Heavenly Father.

14 January

A snow-house has been built a little distance from the ship for the manufacture of candles. When we crossed the equator last June our supply, piled together at the bottom of the hold, became so warm that it formed a shapeless, agglomerate mass of tallow. It is this mass that we are now busily engaged in re-shaping. Having no mould, we make deep cylindrical holes of the correct size in the snow and pour the tallow into these.

Captain McClure and I went out this morning, and returned with noses and cheeks frozen. We have to undergo several days' treatment, and keep to our cabins with masks on. We shall comfort one another. Daily our friendship grows warmer.

31 January

Yesterday the sun reappeared for one minute only, but the sight of it gave new life to the crew. The mercury of the thermometer has frozen repeatedly these last few days. During the month we have enjoyed sixteen appearances of the Aurora Borealis.

5 February

My good mother's birthday. My thoughts went back

with melancholy to the domestic hearth. The captain asked me why I looked so sad, and kindly invited me to supper.

20 February

49 below zero F. We missionaries need to know a little of everything. I busy myself making large felt boots with cork soles for the captain and myself. We shall find them very useful when the lengthening days permit us to hunt.

We are only a short distance from the islet which occupies the middle of the strait, and which we have named Princess Royal Island. The captain, fearing some accident when the ice breaks up, has decided to leave a boat there with provisions for three months. The sailors have levelled a good enough road from the ship to the island, and have marked it with objects of a dark colour [as a guide should anyone be caught on this road in a blizzard].

8 March

When everything had been carried to the island—food, clothing, ammunition, medicines, etc. [including, of course, a large boat], and carefully secured from foxes and bears, the sailors were forbidden to go there. The presence of spirits would expose them to too strong a temptation. [The remains of this cache were visited on May 25th, 1941 by Staff Sergeant H. A. Larsen of the RCMP.]

The snow is dazzling white today: we all wear spectacles of blue glass. The first grindings of the ice make themselves heard. The sound is alarming.

With the coming of April, although the weather was still cold, preparations were made to send out parties to search the shores of Banks and Prince Albert (Victoria) Islands for traces of the lost men of the Franklin expedition. They were to drag their food and tenting equipment on sledges and to stick to the coast-line; for there they might expect to find wreckage, if the ships had been lost, and records, because it was always the practice for Arctic expeditions to leave, preferably at prominent landmarks on the shore-line, records of where they had been and where they expected to go. They would build a pile of stones, called a cairn, and put in it an air-tight cylinder containing a written report. If the travelling parties of the *Investigator* found none of the lost men alive—and after six years there was little likelihood that they would—they hoped at least to learn their fate, and perhaps to find journals and charts recording the discoveries they had made before disaster overtook them.

Chapter six

Journeys over the frozen sea in spring

Y OU WILL remember that when Collinson and McClure left Plymouth on their long voyage to Alaska, another expedition under Captain Austin was preparing to enter the Arctic from the east. It was not to sail until months later, for it had not nearly so far to go, and it was useless to reach the field of search before the summer weather had broken up the ice. Austin's plan was the same as Collinson's—he would sail into the ice as far as he could in the summer of 1850, and in the following spring send out travelling parties to search the adjoining coasts in all directions.

One of his officers, Lieutenant McClintock, spent the months before departure in working out improved methods of sledge travel. He designed sledges and tents to be as light and efficient as possible. He also invented a new kind of alcohol stove for melting snow and making tea. Besides improving equipment, he found a method for making longer journeys possible.

Until then, travel in the Arctic had been almost all by ship; it was not understood that the foot-traveller could keep himself alive, in part at least, by the game he found there. Sledge parties were supposed to depend altogether on the food they carried with them, and when this was half used up they had to give up the search and hurry back to the ship.

McClintock found two ways of lengthening journeys. Beforehand he planted food caches for many miles along the proposed lines of march, which crews could use on the latter part of their return journey. These caches were covered with stones and drenched in water to form a frozen mass which the polar bear could not break into.

Also, he had the outgoing party accompanied for the first part of its journey by a supporting sledge, carrying supplies that fed both crews for many miles and so enabled the main party to make a great part of its outward trip without touching its own load of supplies. By these means men tramping on foot and dragging food and equipment were able to make round journeys of over a thousand miles. McClintock himself, when exploring Eglinton and Prince Patrick Islands, went fourteen hundred—the distance by rail from Montreal to Winnipeg. He also introduced the use of Eskimo dogs, though he never learned to rely on them as the only means of transport, as did later Arctic and Antarctic travellers.

Unfortunately McClure left England before his young friend's ideas had taken shape. His three parties were to travel without caches to rely on, and without supporting sledges. Each of his crews consisted of an officer and six men. They dragged, on a sledge ten feet long, strengthened with iron: a tent eight feet square, with a great skin of buffalo hide to cover it; a sleeping bag for each man; an alcohol lamp, "a precious resource for preparing a hot drink in a few minutes"; various instruments for taking latitude and longitude; guns, ammunition, a few medicines, and, of course, food. The daily ration per man was one pound of salt meat, twelve ounces of sea biscuit, sugar, rum, and cocoa. The men were harnessed to the sledge, while the officer, carrying a double-barrelled gun, telescope, and compass, walked ahead to scout for the easiest way over, or, if possible, around the up-heaved masses of the frozen sea.

Lieutenant Cresswell, in charge of one party, was directed to follow Prince of Wales Strait to its northern outlet, and search the coast of Banks Land to the west. Mr. Wyniatt, mate, was also to ascend the strait, and turning to the right, to explore the shore of Prince Albert Land to the east, beyond Point Peel. The first lieutenant, Haswell, was to go down the strait in the opposite direction and examine the coast of Prince Albert Land to the south and east.

Here McClure made a serious mistake, which came near to costing the life of every man on board. By a mixture of luck and daring he had carried his ship deeper into the Arctic than he or anyone else had expected in one season. He knew that the ice pack, an unpredictable force, varying in its movements from one season to another, might imprison him for years. He knew also that Captain Austin's expedition, coming in from the east, would make every effort to reach Parry's Winter Harbour, less than two hundred miles to the north, in the hope of finding a Franklin record at that famous landmark. So he ought at all costs to have sent a party there to leave notice of his position for Austin to pick up. He was cruelly to regret his failure to do so before twelve months were out.

With part of the crew away, Miertsching redoubled his efforts to teach and evangelize the rest. The officers, good Church of England men, had at first looked on his religious activities with suspicion—at least, so he thought—but seeing that the pious missionary was not trying to make converts, but merely teaching the moral principles common to all branches of the Christian Church, they welcomed his efforts to keep the men occupied through the months of idleness. Had he been a religious teacher only, it is not likely that he would so have won the rough sailors' respect; but he was also a good performer on the guitar, and a hard-working hunter.

"I have been out shooting three times in these last few days," he notes, "and have brought back four hares and twenty-three ptarmigan. On taking stock we find that the *Investigator* has food and fuel for another two years at least. The means of lighting alone are in short supply if we spend another winter like the last. May God avert that!" He did not suspect that they were going to spend not one more winter, but *three,* in the ice which they had entered so light-heartedly.

Although by the end of April the sun had come so far north that daylight was continuous, and the thermometer was sometimes above freezing point, the weather was generally cold and treacherous. An alarming illustration of this occurred early in May.

With the return of daylight, the sporting members of the crew took to hunting vigorously to obtain the fresh meat that was so necessary to ward off the plague of scurvy. As the land on either side of the strait was some miles away, it was usual for hunting parties to carry tent and supplies and to stay away for the night. Mr. Sainsbury, the mate, took half a dozen men to Banks Land, set up the tent, and dismissed his companions to hunt, with the warning that each man should keep at least one comrade in sight.

When a blizzard arose the others found their way back to the tent, but William Whitefield, carpenter's mate, who had over-heated himself in the pursuit of a hare, was seized with giddiness and fell to the ground unconscious. He came to after some hours, almost buried in snow, and with his limbs and organs of speech paralyzed. Though other men could be seen at no great distance searching for him, he had the nightmare experience of being un-able to utter a sound that could reach the rescuers' ears. His struggles, however, stimulated the action of the heart, and as his comrades moved away and disappeared from sight, he was able to crawl after them.

The men had returned to the tent to be re-mustered, as a pre-caution against more casualties, for the weather was still thick and blustery. They were taking hot tea before going out again, when they were struck speechless by the cry that a polar bear was upon them. Listening intently, they heard the sound of some heavy body dragging itself across the snow; and they knew that it was the habit of the polar bear thus to approach when stalking a seal. They all seized their firearms, while one man cautiously opened the flap of the tent.

> Instead of a bear the appalling spectacle of their miss-ing comrade met his view. The poor fellow had crawled within a couple of yards of the tent, when he was unable to proceed one step farther; he could not speak, his body rested on his hands and knees, the head thrown back, the eyes fixed and immovable, the nose, mouth, and ears filled with snow, which was fast accumulating about him; the jaws and limbs rigid. He was instantly dragged into

the tent; Sainsbury could feel no pulse, a slight movement of the chest being the only indication of life.

Warm blankets, chafing of the limbs, and a little rum restored him to consciousness, and Mr. Piers, assistant surgeon, in response to an urgent summons, came with a sledge and carried him to the ship, frost-bitten and delirious. Few men have had so narrow an escape from freezing to death.

On May 20th Lieutenant Cresswell and his party came back after an outing of thirty days. They reported that after rounding Cape Russell they had been assailed by fierce gales blowing from the north-west down Melville Sound, but had attained a distance of a hundred and seventy miles from the ship, and reached an area which they and their mates were to know too well in the winters to come. There several men had been frost-bitten; and fearing that they would become unfit for work, Cresswell turned back just when improved weather promised good travelling.

It was well that he did so, for frozen fingers and toes became gangrenous. In spite of their protests, Cresswell put two of the men on the sledge, and took their place at the drag-ropes for the rest of the homeward journey. The sailmaker, Facey, had some fingers and toes amputated; but notwithstanding that he afterwards served in men-of-war with Dr. Armstrong in the Baltic and the West Indies, and, the surgeon records, could always predict changes in the weather from the pain he felt in his stumps.

Cresswell reported high sandstone cliffs on the north shore of Banks Land, and out to sea "stupendous ice". His mates were to know all about that also. They were surprised at his assertion that he had detected a seam of coal in the rock. They could not have supposed that a hundred years later the land they found so worthless and desolate would be marked out for an oil survey.

Nine days later Haswell returned from his exploration southward, along the shore of Prince Albert (now Victoria) Island. Like Cresswell, he had found no trace of the lost ships; but he had, though for years he did not know it, almost met the great traveller, Dr. John Rae, who had come up from a Hudson Bay trading post to search the south shore of Victoria Island on foot and by boat.

Haswell informed McClure that eight days' journey to the south he had met a group of eighteen Eskimos catching seal in the ice cracks, which were beginning to open in the milder weather. The natives had been friendly, and had readily traded sealskins for buttons, but, in the absence of an interpreter, could not be questioned about Franklin. McClure at once decided to take Miertsching and a sledge party to pay these folk a visit. They made a rapid journey, and on the third day, on coming over a hill (travel by land was easier now in some places, as the sea ice was flooded with melting snow), they saw on the beach a cluster of tents with Eskimos coming and going around them. Writes Miertsching:

> I was as happy and excited as one who, after a long separation, is about to meet his fellow-countrymen again. Would we understand one another? I approached them. As soon as I was within earshot I shouted: "We are friends; we bring you gifts." They remained silent, staring at us with uneasiness. At last they all cried out together, "Sivoragut." Oh, happiness! It was the language, the intonation, of my friends in Labrador. The word means "we are afraid". They did not adopt a posture of defence, but awaited our approach motionless and stupefied. They had never seen strangers, and might well think us superhuman beings.

Miertsching, one should note, is apt to colour his narrative too highly. The Eskimos had seen Lieutenant Haswell and his men a few days before.

> Habits, language, complexion, tools, all reminded me of my Labrador friends. They seemed much surprised when I told them that the world contained great and populous countries. They had supposed that they and their neighbours were the only people in the world. After

having conversed with them for a while, I spread before them, at the Captain's request, a sheet of paper on which I had sketched our ship, and the coast-line between her and our present position; and asked them to continue the sketch. I had great difficulty in making them comprehend what I wished; when they understood, they traced a map with more skill than I would have thought possible. All the natives, men and women, approached with curiosity, and declared that it was most exact. They extended the map as far as Cape Parry; the well-known islands of Sutton and Liston in Dauphin [Dolphin and Union] Strait were so correctly indicated that we had confidence in those features that were new to us.

Miertsching appears not to have known that on earlier voyages Parry and Ross found the Eskimos to be well-informed and skilful geographers.

Whilst Captain McClure and the sailors were visiting the dwellings, I conversed with their occupants in the open air. Their notions of religion were the same as those of the Eskimos of Cape Bathurst. Among them also I found the tradition of the Flood, which is preserved in varying degrees of distortion among all peoples. In the interior of the country a mountain rears its head, on which their ancestors had pitched their tents during an inundation. I tried to appeal to their consciences, and spoke to them of God and His mercy. We became good friends, and I heaved a great sigh when the Captain gave the signal for departure.

I distributed the usual gifts—knives, saws, red and blue handkerchiefs, and glass beads. Small mirrors excited them beyond measure. They could not rid themselves of the idea that it was our wish to exchange goods, and kept on asking: "What ought we to give in return?"

Our adieux were said and the sledge in motion when Captain McClure, his heart moved at the thought of quitting these simple folk whom we would never see again, turned back, and, noticing a young mother poorly dressed with her child inside her jacket, took off his downy scarf of red wool and ran to throw it over her shoulders. Perplexed and troubled, the young woman looked around as if seeking something, then took her child, kissed it repeatedly, and offered it to Captain Mc-Clure. When I had made her understand that the captain was making her a gift—a wholly gratuitous gift—she began to kiss her child anew with a rapturous expression which seemed to say, "Then I may keep you too!"

Then, fingering the flannel, she asked me of what animal it was the skin. Never having seen any fabric, they supposed that our clothes, as well as the canvas of our tent, and our paper, were the skins of different species of wild beast.

How much I had to say to them! How interesting it would have been to stay there for some days; what joy it would have been to tell them of their Heavenly Father, of Jesus, the friend of the lowly, and to do good to their souls! I think that we all had tears in our eyes on departing. Who can imagine the marvellous traditions of which we shall be the heroes in time to come? May God hasten the day when the bearers of the good tidings of salvation reach this desolate country.

The white men did not remain the vague tradition of a lonely tribe as long as Miertsching expected. He underestimated the rate of progress in the American North-west. A few years later the United States Government was to purchase the territory of Alaska from Russia; and the lure of the whale fisheries and of gold was to bring men flocking to Alaska, to the Klondike, and into the adjoining seas. At the turn of the century American whalers were wintering regularly at Herschel Island near the Mackenzie, with a detachment of the Canadian Mounted Police to keep them in order, and to protect the natives from ill-usage.

In 1906, when Roald Amundsen passed by on his great voyage through the Passage, and when the young anthropologist, Vilhjalmur Stefansson, was on the Mackenzie delta, getting his first experience of life among the Eskimos, there still dwelt on Victoria Island an old Eskimo woman who told of the coming of the first White Chief and of the kindness he had done her.

On the return journey the travellers were caught in a blizzard on the 4th of June, and for some hours lost their way amongst a maze of crevasses. On reaching the ship McClure took to his bed, seriously ill. The next day Wyniatt came back with the last of the searching parties. After emerging from the north end of Prince of Wales Strait he had, in obedience to his orders, turned to the east and made a long survey of the north shore of Victoria Island.

> Everywhere they found Eskimo homes, evidently long deserted. On a little mossy plain were scattered the ruins of thirty-two stone erections. But nothing—absolutely nothing!—of poor Franklin.

Chapter seven

"We shall go right on to the end."

WHEN WYNIATT at this farthest point gave the order to turn back, he did not suspect that Lieutenant Sherard Osborn of the eastern expedition was camping barely sixty miles away on the other side of the unknown strait that was later to bear the name of McClintock Channel.

Captain Austin had quitted England in the spring of the previous year, and with two ships of the *Investigator* type and two steam tenders had safely passed through Lancaster Sound. On Beechey Island, near the entrance of Wellington Channel, were found traces of Franklin's winter quarters for 1845-46; but as no cairn containing notice of his intended movements was anywhere to be seen, the search was not much advanced by this discovery. In pursuit of his original plan, Austin tried to push west through Barrow Strait to Melville Sound, but was frozen in, far short of his objectives, at Griffiths Island, near the modern station of Resolute Bay.

In the spring of 1851 sledge parties organized and equipped by McClintock set out in various directions—Osborn, as we have seen, reached down the west coast of Prince of Wales Island. McClintock made the four-hundred-mile tramp to Melville Island and Winter Harbour, and there left the customary metal cylinder, giving notice of his visit. He did not suspect, as he swept the horizon to the south-west with his telescope, that he was close to the sledge tracks of Cresswell and Wyniatt, and that just under the skyline lay the ship of his friend McClure. He brought back word that he had seen not a trace of any expedition, old or new. McClure's failure to send a party to Winter Harbour was bearing fruit.

For the *Investigators* there remained nothing to do but watch the slow advance of summer, and await the break-up of the ice, which they knew must still be some weeks away. The snow disappeared from the land; the torrents of spring died away to mere trickles. The sea ice was more resistant, though the upheaved hummocks were turning yellow and crumbling at the edges. Beyond them, on either side of the strait, a more varied landscape was replacing the monotonous white of winter. Valleys here and there showed streaks of grey, where the snow never melted, but on sunny slopes the Arctic vegetation was displaying a short-lived radiance of colour.

> The lovely golden hue of the anemone and the poppy, the purple-blossomed saxifrage, and the white violets of the London-pride appear interlaced with the rich green of the ground-willow and the rose-tinted leaves of sorrel; all relieve the wanderer's eye, and carry him back with softened feelings to some nook in his own dear land, where the flowers, and trees, and herbs, though far surpassing in loveliness those before him, are yet not half so much appreciated.

Wild-fowl were there in profusion—ducks of various kinds and the Brent goose made their nest, "in spite of the fox and the piratical boatswain-bird, the former in quest of the parent, and the latter of her eggs". And along the base of the sunlit cliffs, where the water first appeared, "clouds of shrieking gulls, kittiwakes, and burgomasters hold a noisy parliament. There was no night to overshadow this scene: the sun rose high during the day along the southern half of the heavens, and sloped without setting towards the north until midnight. There was no darkness now, as, during the winter, there had been no light."

Though given up to idleness and sentimental musing, the adventurers were ready to seize any chance of a more manly occupation. On June 10th Miertsching wrote:

> After breakfast the look-out reported a white bear some distance off. With our glasses we could distinctly

make out his black eyes and the movements of his head. Taking our guns we ventured forth valiantly across the snow and through the puddles of water. When we were within fifty paces, the bear vanished from sight. We greeted his departure with a Homeric burst of laughter. It was one of those mirages with which the Polar traveller is so familiar.

24 June

My dear captain has been quite indisposed since our journey. He has a bad cold. Perhaps the scarf which he gave the young Eskimo woman was badly missed, but I am sure he does not regret it. I spend hours and hours with him; we read; we talk; every day strengthens our mutual understanding. Oh! how friendship adds charm to life! God be thanked for this pleasant relationship.

All is ready for departure. We are waiting impatiently for the ice to set us free.

Miertsching and his shipmates had another three weeks to wait after the making of the impatient entry just noted. The sea ice, where the accumulated cold of the long winter was stored up, was the last to yield to the season; and it was July 10th, when the peak of summer was past, before it began to break up and drift away to the south. In less than a week her crew had got the ship under way, with the eager hope that a few days would see them out of the strait, and across Melville Sound into the homeward track of Sir Edward Parry.

14 July

Thunderous crashings are heard. The ship is in motion. After ten months' silence the word of command resounds. The captain, barely convalescent, has insisted on being brought on deck. Seals in great numbers accompany the ship, and amuse us with their gambollings.

16 July

We continue to move. The wind drives us with force. The movement of the ice is such as it was last night—in a moment three stout anchors have been broken. Blocks of more than half a ton in weight are piled up in heaps, which then collapse with the roar of an avalanche.

To the south, along Prince of Wales Strait, lay loose "sailing ice", and McClure was perfectly free to go back the way he had come. But his mind was set on carrying his ship home through the Passage he had discovered; so until the ice to the north should open up enough to afford a free passage, he anchored his ship to a floe and drifted north with the wind. The Princess Royal Islands passed slowly out of sight, and many were the prayers uttered that they might never again be seen.

> 21 July
> The crew is wearied with handling the ship; to rest them the captain gives the order to anchor. The anchors are fixed in a floe which we have the curiosity to measure. We find it five miles by two, with a depth of sixty feet.

Ten days later they had made little progress and were still in trouble:

> 31 July
> A barrier of ice again blocks our progress. We try to open a way with explosives. But the expenditure of two hundredweight of powder having enabled us to progress one mile only in three hours, we give up and prefer to wait.

For a whole month the officers and men of the *Investigator* tried every means in their power to work their ship to the north. They had no mind for another winter in the Arctic—one way or another they must get home. Behind them the sea lay open and unhampered; but to return by that route meant the troublesome navigation along the Alaskan shore, and an ocean voyage of many months. If they could only burst through the barrier of ice that lay ahead, the journey home was a matter of weeks only; Parry had proved that. So, though hindered by intermittent rain and fog, they blasted away, hoisted out the boats to tow, or got the ship ahead in short stages by warping—that is, anchoring her with a long cable to a solid mass ahead and winding her up with the capstan.

For four days they drifted blindly in the fog, and when it lifted found that they were at the outlet of the strait, with Cape Russell plainly visible on the left hand and Cape Peel on the right. They were on the margin of Melville Sound, which for nearly a year had been the object of all their endeavours. But on its surface lay, not the broken and moving pack that they had looked for, but a field of ice which had not even the appearance of breaking up. The captain mounted to the crow's-nest and found that "this solid plain extends as far as the eye can follow it—no hope whatever of making Barrow Strait by this route."

It was now mid-August. Nearly half the season of navigation was over; the sun was receding and already dipping below the northern horizon at midnight. McClure saw that to persevere in his effort was likely to mean a second winter berth within forty miles of his first. So he gave orders to put about, and sailed back down the strait where so much labour had been spent in vain. They passed the Princess Royal Islands, which they had hoped never to see again, and with a strong following breeze found themselves next morning again approaching Nelson Head.

The voyage of the *Investigator* was a series of accidents. Accident had separated her from the *Enterprise* and launched her on an independent cruise. Three times that spring, accident had prevented her from making her position known to other expeditions, and kept her in dangerous isolation. And now again chance decreed that she should plunge even deeper into the perilous seas from which she had just escaped. If McClure, on emerging from the strait, had found the south shore of Banks Land badly ice-infested, he would, no doubt, have returned to the Canadian mainland and made a peaceful exit by way of Alaska, as Collinson did after him. But the treacherous seas on which he was embarked offered a lure which the daring Irishman was the last man in the world to resist. As the ocean broadened out beyond

Nelson Head, he could make out only a faint margin of ice on the southern skyline; the ship herself was in a wide expanse of open water, pitching as she had not pitched since leaving the Pacific, and plunging her bows into the rollers, until the water washed back as far as the fore-hatch. He was free to steer in whatever direction he chose; and his choice was quickly made. Banks Land was of unknown extent, but probably not too large: he would endeavour to sail around it, enter Melville Sound from the west, and carry his ship through the Northwest Passage after all.

For a day or two all went well. With a stiff following breeze the *Investigator* ploughed steadily ahead, and soon arrived off Point Kellett. There Mr. Court took a boat in shore and found a small but convenient haven, later to be the Sachs Harbour where Vilhjalmur Stefansson rejoined his ship after his famous drift on an ice-cake across the Beaufort Sea. From there the coast pointed a little to the east of north, and McClure was encouraged to believe that Banks Land was a small island which could be circumnavigated in a few days. But to the north-west the dreaded ice-blink reappeared, and soon very heavy pack came in sight, bearing down as threateningly as ever.

McClure did not suspect that he was leading his men into a death-trap. He had no experience to guide him. Until then British discovery ships had sailed among the islands in more or less narrow channels, where the ice seldom reached a thickness of more than six or seven feet; for it was broken up every year by the force of tide and current, and drifted out through Baffin Bay to melt away in the Atlantic. But the *Investigator* was sailing outside the farthest island, into that part of the Arctic called the Beaufort Sea.

Its spacious surface was unbroken by land, and there the ice grew year after year to a thickness of perhaps sixty feet. Caught in its cruel web, a ship had no chance. In 1879 the American steamer *Jeannette* was to venture into it. She was unreported for three years, and then the body of her captain, the heroic De Long, was found in a snowdrift near the Lena Delta. A few of his crew were rescued by Siberian natives, to tell the story of a ship imprisoned and dragged away for twenty months, and then ground to pieces by the jagged floes.

In 1913 the Canadian discovery ship *Karluk* was beset off Alaska and drifted out to sea. Her captain, Bob Bartlett, was the greatest Arctic navigator of his day; he had been Robert Peary's right-hand man, and had accompanied him almost to the Pole. Nothing could stop him then; but he met his Waterloo in the Beaufort Sea. Bartlett and some of his men escaped to land; but the ship and eleven of her company were left behind in the deadly embrace of the ice.

Guessing nothing of this, and supposing that the heavy ice was a local accident and not part of a vast pattern, McClure held to his course and coasted fearlessly up the west shore of Banks Land. At first he did so with ease and safety. The coast he was following resembled that of northern Alaska; the sea bottom sloped gently away, and the ice, with a far greater depth than the ship, grounded three miles from the shore. The fragments that flaked off and drifted in shore were too small and scattered to cause any trouble. But this did not last. On rounding Cape Prince Alfred the explorers came upon a bolder, rockier coast, where the cliffs, plunging steeply into the sea, allowed the ice to float in shore and narrow the gap between it and the beach.

"We are sailing along a veritable canal," wrote Miertsching, "bordered on the right hand by Baring [Banks] Land, on the left by a regular continent of Polar ice. One would say that the canal had been prepared for us. Sometimes our margin of safety is so narrow that projecting angles of ice have to be blasted away. We have no idea of how all this will end."

They were not long in finding out. On the morning of August 20th the ice was found lying so close in shore that progress was no longer possible. The *Investigator* crept inside a grounded floe of such tremendous size that she found a depth of fifty feet in its lee, anchored herself to the ice in order not to drift ashore, and waited for a wind that might drive back the pack and reopen a passage.

On the one side was an immense field of ice rising to a uniform twelve feet above the level of the sea, on the other a bleak and rocky shore without trace of bay or cove to shelter the ship from a westerly gale. A strong wind from that quarter might easily set the ice-filled sea in motion, and with the monstrous force of millions upon millions of tons, drive the grounded ice up the sloping escarpment of the sea bottom, and either ride the ship down or crush her against the rocks of Banks Land.

It was a bitter disappointment for the crew. They had been under sail for four days only, yet they had all but circumnavigated Banks Land; for they had, as they supposed, arrived at the strait, now named after McClure, that opens into Melville Sound from the west. The trend of the coast beyond Cape Alfred pointed direct to Winter Harbour, now barely two hundred miles away. *There* they would be on the homeward trail blazed by Parry thirty years before; *here* they were in worse plight than in Prince of Wales Strait; for they were in greater danger, and had thrown away their one chance of retreat.

Chapter eight

Stopped at last

HOWEVER, THEY were learning to make the best of their lot, whatever it might happen to be. At any rate, Dr. Armstrong observed, in their winter quarters they had been miles from land; here they were only a few feet away—a comforting thought for a man of science, though not altogether a soothing reflection for a sailor.

They made the most of their opportunities. Armstrong and Miertsching, though divided on some questions, shared an interest in botany. They went out plant-collecting, and climbed to the top of a mountain that reared its head not far from the ship. "Our melancholy gaze takes in nothing as far as the skyline except a sea of ice, dotted here and there by the uprearing of enormous blocks." The poor interpreter remembered that it was his birthday; he thought of his mother, and his eyes filled with tears.

No wonder he felt lonely. On that August afternoon of 1851, as the German pastor and the Irish surgeon gazed out over the ice-cap—which, as they guessed, and we know, extended without interruption as far as the Pole—southern Alaska was the home of a few seal-fisheries, the lure of gold was just beginning to attract settlers to British Columbia, Winnipeg was a frontier trading-post. They were many thousands of miles from civilization, and for aught they knew, they were the only ship in the Arctic. Perhaps never in history have pioneers advanced so far beyond the frontiers of settlement as McClure's tramp freighter and the sixty-six stout-hearts who manned her.

On getting back to the ship, they learned that the mate and the assistant surgeon had made a find of great interest—fossilized trees. Armstrong and McClure at once set out in the whale-boat to confirm this remarkable discovery. They landed and ascended a ravine, where, about a quarter of a mile from the beach and three hundred feet above the level of the sea, they came upon a hillside full of trees buried in its soil in various stages of petrifaction. A piece seven feet long and three in circumference was brought on board. When the ship was later abandoned a fragment of this was saved and placed in Dublin Museum. It showed a strange alteration of climate, Armstrong thought, that stately trees once grew where now the dwarf willow struggles for existence.

Hunting excursions deeper into the country met with little success; "but bones of various species and ruined dwellings make us believe that the climate was milder formerly. How far back is that 'formerly'?" asks Miertsching. "A long way, no doubt; for this climate preserves for a long time even those substances which are most liable to decay."

August 29th was near to being the last day of that long and adventurous cruise. The danger that the travellers feared most— a gale from the west with snow and sleet—assailed them. Miertsching told the story thus:

> This is a day which I will never forget to the end of my life. The day before yesterday a deep grumbling in the ice warned us of a distant storm. Under its impulse the ice began to heave like the ground in an earthquake. The uproar was appalling. The ship was tossed this way and that. From 2 A.M. until evening we never quitted the deck, but stood in our warmest clothing, holding little bundles of indispensable articles, like people about to set out on a journey. The ship, raised slowly to a certain height, fell suddenly on her broadside, and then righted to repeat the same evolution, like the death-agony of a tortured animal. The long beams cracked and groaned; the cabin doors emitted a sharper note. The captain preserved a remarkable composure, but at 6 P.M. I heard him exclaim: "Now it is all over; in five minutes we shall

have no ship!" I remembered that God often sends deliverance only when things have come to the worst, and a ray of hope entered my heart.

Armstrong coolly narrates:

> We lay not only helplessly fixed, but absolutely embedded, borne along amidst the appalling commotion of huge masses grinding and crushing each other, and still nearing the shore, and approaching the berg, from which we were not more than a few feet distant. Every man stood firm and silent at his post, with a knapsack at his side. The sick I had ordered to be brought on deck, that in event of the ship being suddenly crushed, they too might have a chance to escape. Nothing was heard except the dismal sound of the ice around us. We slowly but steadily approached the berg, against which our stern post at length came in contact. The pressure continuing, every timber of the ship's solid framework loudly complained, and we momentarily expected to see her nipped in pieces or thrown upon the beach.

Naturally preferring the latter alternative, McClure gave orders to cast off the hawsers that bound her to the floe, when the wind began to subside, and the ocean swell, under that monstrous weight of ice, immediately died away. "A solemn silence succeeded to the uproar. We eyed one another without breathing. I hope that some remembered to return thanks. The captain requested us all to remain at our posts, withdrew to his cabin, and then returned to give his orders with much calm and dignity."

Though she had escaped immediate destruction, the position of the ship was one of greater danger than ever. She had been driven hundreds of yards along the beach, from a depth of eight fathoms to one of three and a half; she was thrown up and lying over at an angle of eighteen degrees. Work with axe and saw, and a cautious use of blasting powder, put her back in an upright position; but she was cradled in the ice that had been forced under her keel, and was a sitting duck for the next storm.

It was now September, and the brief period of arctic navigation was clearly over. McClure therefore sent men up and down the beach to pick up driftwood, and detailed others to gather rocks for ballast, which the ship, lightened by the consumption of supplies, would soon need—hence the scene of this detention was named Ballast Beach. The weather continued cold, raw, and snowy, confirming the belief that, unsatisfactory as their berth was, they could hope for no better. On September the 10th, however, the wind veered to the south and then to the east, bringing higher temperatures, and producing clefts in the ice as the pack began to ease off shore. But, perched as they were on a grounded ice cake, the crew were powerless to make use of the opportunity which this offered.

The deliverance they had ceased to hope for was unexpectedly granted them. Throughout their detention at Ballast Beach the watch had taken regular tidal observations at a pole set up beside the ship. Descending at dead of night to take a reading, a petty officer was astonished to see the tide-pole slowly moving away from him. Then he realized that their ice-dock was in motion, silently floating out to the open sea.

Morning found the ship drifting eastward at the rate of about a mile an hour. Small charges of powder freed her from her icy sheath, but in the afternoon she was again driven in shore by a high wind and the returning pack, and was made fast to grounded ice. The danger was not as acute as it had been at Ballast Beach, for the *Investigator* was now aground on the north shore of Banks Land, and the eastward-moving pack was travelling parallel to the land instead of driving into it. But there was always the danger that the inner edge of a moving floe might catch on the shore ice or the sea bottom, pivot landwards, and with all the force of the gale behind it, and with the leverage of its great length, drive the ship from her anchorage up on to the beach.

Through the long, dark night, the sullen grinding of the moving pack, and the loud report made by some huge mass of ice which burst under the pressure, boomed through the solitude, and as the starlight glimmered over the wild scene to seaward, the men could just detect the pack rearing up and rolling over, by the alternate reflected lights and shadows.

Daylight found them safe and undisturbed; a lane gradually opened before them, and they again ventured to quit their anchorage and sail east towards the long-sought Melville Island, through an avenue formed by the shore ice on the one hand and the moving pack on the other.

> Making a little headway this last few days, we reached the cape which receives the name of Crozier, and rises perpendicularly three hundred feet. Today is Sunday. The Service is celebrated, according to custom, by reading the Liturgy and a portion of the Bible. I am growing attached to this form of worship which our captain performs with a solemn simplicity. The seamen appear more seriously disposed than they were recently. Agonising fear and deliverance have turned the thoughts of several towards "the hills whence cometh our aid."

The sailors had other reasons for appearing serious, for they were terribly overworked; they were continually either adjusting the sails to manoeuvre the ship along a crooked ice lane, lowering the boats to take her in tow, or running out cables to warp her clear of a threatened jam. Once they had to cut and blast out an "ice-dock" where the ship could hide from a threatened nip. When not employed they were often kept on deck for fear of the crises that might develop in a moment, and were issued with extra rations and grog to make up for the lack of sleep. But it was a maxim of the British sailor's that on his low wage-scale, it was not for him to worry—"the officer is paid for thinking"; and it appears from a story Miertsching tells us that they took even the strange and unfamiliar dangers of the Banks Land cruise quite coolly.

> Although we see ice only, and the look-out in the crow's-nest repeats incessantly, "ice, ice," nevertheless we

continue to make headway at the rate of ten knots. [This seems an exaggeration.] We are confined, as last month, to a narrow channel—so narrow that whenever the ship rolls a little more heavily than usual the masts strike on the walls of ice which serve as parapets on the right hand and the left. I think of the Children of Israel passing through the Red Sea.

This evening in conversation a bearded old sailor began to talk: "My mother used to read a great book and tell us marvellous tales of times gone by, of men changed into stone, of ramparts crumbling at the sound of the trumpet. They had no ships in those days. Thousands of people crossed the English Channel on foot, the waters having parted to give them passage. It was then that England was peopled. My poor mother said that since the time of Richard the Lionheart such miracles have not occurred and will never occur again. What is she going to say when I tell her what I have seen with my own eyes?"

This brave sailor, zealous and exact in the performance of his duties, was born in Christian England, he was baptised there, and there he grew up!

Miertsching and the sailor whose garbling of Scripture so shocked the pious missionary could look without panic on the dangers that surrounded them, but the nerve of the officers on whom they relied was beginning to give way under the incessant strain of this critical navigation. Continues Miertsching:

> I was standing near the captain, when the ice-mate descended without permission from the crow's-nest, and approached him. Pale and with a trembling voice he excused himself, saying that he had not the strength to endure such a spectacle any longer: "Ice, captain, nothing but ice. As far as the eye can reach I do not see a spoonful of water, and yet we are moving forward all the time. I cannot bring myself to go aloft again!"

This poor pilot had the expression of one who had just seen a spectre. Children and grown-ups alike, when we are confronted by the strange and the monstrous, we need to huddle together.

We are not told what reply the captain made to the ice-master. Probably he suspended him from his duties, placed him under arrest, and released him the next day when the ship was in winter quarters, and the example he had set could no longer do harm.

September 23rd, the last day of that fantastic cruise, dawned most hopefully. The ship had passed Capes Austin and Crozier, the northernmost points of Banks Land, which, projecting into McClure Strait, edged the drifting pack away from the land, and formed a stretch of open water to the east. Under full sail the *Investigator* was making rapid progress, and the officers were laying bets that the next day would see them at Melville Island, now barely a hundred miles away.

But it was the fate of the *Investigator* to miss both disaster and success by the narrowest possible margin. Towards evening the wind freshened, with squalls of snow; fog hid the coast of Banks Land, the edge of the pack to seaward was barely visible through the gloom. Fearing that the ice was closing in, and to take all possible advantage of the open water while it lasted, McClure kept on under full sail through the gathering darkness. The leadsman had just reported fifteen fathoms when the ship struck a sand-bank with such violence that she remained fast, with her bows thrown up eight feet.

If the pack came down on her in this situation, her destruction was certain. Everyone understood that; so orders were obeyed with promptitude and zeal. Cargo was shifted to the stern and some hoisted out and stacked on the ice. Anchors were then laid out astern, and all ranks strained at the capstan; but the ship would not budge.

At the bows the lead gave us five feet only, instead of the sixteen necessary to float us. Such efforts were made that, in spite of the temperature, our clothes were dripping with sweat. All the seamen were exhausted. The captain sounded the retreat, and, as I was going to my cabin, he said to me; "When you have changed your clothes come and have a cup of tea with me."

When I entered his cabin, he rose, and, pointing to an open book, said not without bitterness: "See how this passage in the Bible corresponds to our situation. In this agonizing hour, when our lives hang by a thread, I wished to do as you do. I opened the Word of God, praying that He would let me find consolation, and see what the reply is." He pointed to verses 2 and 3 of Psalm XXXIV:

"O magnify the Lord with me and let us exalt his name together.

"I sought the Lord and he heard me, and delivered me out of all my fears."

I read this passage aloud. Captain McClure broke in: "I understand *our* situation only too well." "Sometimes," I replied, "these responses of Holy Writ have seemed to me, as they seem now to you, a delusion and a mockery; later the event has justified them."

We sat down face to face and were drinking our tea in silence when we felt a terrific shock. Quicker than lightning McClure was on deck; when I overtook him the *Investigator* was floating with ease. An ice-floe had done what all our united exertions had failed to accomplish. Driven under the bow by the wind, or rather by the mighty hand of God, it had in a moment jarred the ship free. Need I describe the feelings in the hearts of all on board, especially in the Captain's and mine?

The ice, says Armstrong, struck the ship on her broadside towards the stern and instantly pried her clear of the mud-bank in which she was embedded. She re-anchored in six fathoms, and the men set to work retrieving supplies from the ice on which they had been thrown, re-stowing the cargo, and giving order to the confusion which the near shipwreck had created. That night no one slept. Armstrong's calm narrative reads:

> As midnight came, the night wore as wild and tempestuous an aspect as any of us had, perhaps, ever seen at sea. The wind had increased to a gale from the westward, which, while it brought some heavy loose ice about us, kept the pack off shore; the snowy whiteness of the former presenting a strange feature in the scene, looming ominously in the darkness; while the cold raw atmosphere, the howling of the wind, the darkness of the night, and the chance there existed of the pack setting down on us, assisted to form a picture of Arctic cruising, which I cannot fully describe, but can never cease to remember.

The next day was the fatal day of decision. The gale abated with the approach of dawn, and clear daylight revealed the *Investigator,* battered but seaworthy as ever, bobbing up and down and tugging at her anchors in the swell. The sand-bar on which she had been all but wrecked was now seen to be the submerged extension of a cape on the western angle of an ice-free inlet running many miles back into the land. It was seven miles across at its mouth, and its eastern limit was marked by another cape, Point Back. At McClure's orders Mr. Court embarked in the whaleboat, sounded his way around the end of the submerged spit, and piloted the ship into the harbour so unexpectedly found, the "Bay of Mercy". It was now September 24th, so here the Captain resolved to winter. He anchored three miles inside the sand-bar and gave his men rest after thirty hours of continuous labour.

The landlocked arctic harbour was apt to prove a treacherous host. Being sheltered from ocean currents and the full force of the winds, it might remain a sheet of ice for several seasons, unless a summer gale arose from the right quarter to shatter its sodden, half-melted surface and drive the broken masses out to sea. Thus the ship that put into it for the winter might be imprisoned for years. It was precisely this that happened to the *Investigator:* she was in the Bay of Mercy to stay.

Chapter nine

Through the polar night

Armstrong was bitterly critical of his captain for so ending the summer's cruise—"the fatal error of our voyage," he asserts. Across the mouth of the bay, he says, to Point Back, which marked its eastern extremity, lay loose "sailing ice", and beyond the cape, as Mr. Court found out later, lay perfectly open sea. In McClure's opinion the ice lay so close against Point Back that he could not round it. Had he known that the sea beyond was open, he might have made the attempt; but by the time he received Court's report, the still waters of the bay were frozen to a thickness that made it impossible for the ship to move again that season.

If Armstrong was right—and some of the ship's officers, he says, shared his opinion—it was a tragic decision on McClure's part not to push on. Had he reached Melville Island that autumn, he would certainly have got out through Barrow Strait in the following summer, for it was then that the ships sent to his rescue achieved the more difficult task of getting in. In our own century the Northwest Passage has been navigated, not without difficulty, by Amundsen's *Gjoa* and the RCMP schooner *St. Roch,* both small engined craft. To have carried the *Investigator* through—a much larger vessel, with sail only—would have won for the British Navy the honour it has fairly earned by its work in the Canadian Arctic, and have given McClure rank among the great navigators of history.

It is quite possible that in a moment of extreme exhaustion and discouragement the bold captain missed by a hairbreadth the exploit that he had braved so many dangers to accomplish. The harrowing experience at Ballast Beach may have wrecked his self-confidence. Armstrong, a prejudiced but by no means contemptible witness, repeatedly accuses him of irresolution in the critical days from September 10th to September 24th.

Yet no one has a right to blame him for the course he chose. If Miertsching's narrative is to be trusted, one of his officers was suffering from a nervous breakdown; the men, continuously on duty for thirty hours, under a great strain (as Armstrong admits) for several days, cannot have been much better; so it is no wonder that the captain failed to adjust his course to a sudden opportunity, if Armstrong is right and the opportunity was there. McClure himself was of the opinion that it was not. The delay at the sand-bar, he thought, had been fatal to success; while the ship was aground the gap in the ice-stream had moved too far to the east; when she was refloated it was twelve hours too late. In no case is it fair to blame him for going no farther, when few men would have gone so far.

A few days after the ship was embayed, Mr. Court was sent east with a party to connect the Bay of Mercy with Lieutenant Cresswell's "farthest" on his sledge journey in the spring. He did this in three days, and the map of the Banks Land coast was complete. It was then that Court observed open water across Melville Sound. His own opinion of the captain's action is not recorded.

Preparations were now made for winter. Housing was again stretched over the upper deck, and a mammoth wash-day was held before the cold became too severe. Stock-taking revealed a quantity of spoiled provisions, and in consequence rations were reduced by one-third. The second winter was going to be much harder than the first.

31 October [1851]

On the 26th we celebrated the anniversary of the discovery of the Passage a year ago. The crew were given grog and a full ration. The sailors organized games and dances, which they performed for our entertainment. In acknowledgement of their compliments the captain said that he hoped in a few months to cross the new passage which separates us from Melville Island, and thus we may all go home together to observe this anniversary in England. In the meantime the season's ice [boy ice] is already eighteen inches thick, and the thermometer at eighteen degrees below zero!

7 November

The sun shone for three minutes only yesterday. Farewell until February!

29 November

This winter is passing pretty much like last year's. But the one-third reduction in rations, which, at a distance, may appear trivial, has in the long run great importance. Our sailors are incapable of the somewhat violent exertions by which they keep themselves warm. They go walking up and down the level esplanade near the ship, and come in quite worn out. Night school interests them.

The same dampness from which we suffered so much has again become our torment. The hot shot which have appeared once more in our cabins do not dry them perfectly. Oh! to sleep one night in a dry bed. What a delight!

December 6

The captain, to clarify his suspicions, has made a fresh and very careful examination of our supplies. As he feared several cases, that were believed good, have spoiled. Henceforth we shall be on half rations. Candles are in very short supply: order is given to reserve them for cases of necessity. Therefore we spend the greater part of the twenty-four-hour night in utter darkness. Next to no reading; inappeasable hunger! Walking and sleeping our only resources. The wolves make themselves heard all around with dismal howling. During my solitary walks my heart goes out to my well-beloved far away in the Fatherland, and the tears run down my cheeks.

31 December

Young ice is three feet, eight inches thick. Christmas was joyously celebrated as in our families in Europe. Full rations, plum pudding, and an ungrudging supply of candles. This last luxury was not the least enjoyable.

Sober-minded persons might perhaps be disposed to find fault with this; but let them reflect that, if ever a feast is desirable to break monotony, it is in a situation like ours.

31 January [1852]

What to write in this journal, which has been interrupted for a month, except that we have been very cold, very hungry, and that three men have been punished for robbing the watch-dogs of their food? Thickness of new ice four feet eight inches: fifty below zero.

4 February

We enjoy today an hour's twilight, which will grow daily in duration and brightness. Soon the sun will reappear; and, like overgrown children, we play as to who shall be the first to see it. Hunting has recommenced, but it is dangerous, for darkness comes on so quickly.

As Miertsching's mournful narrative suggests, the second winter was much more trying than the first. The Bay of Mercy was a deep inlet, running thirteen miles into the land, but McClure had naturally, with an eye to getting the ship out easily, taken her no further in than seemed necessary for her safety, and she was more exposed to northerly winds than she had been in Prince of Wales Strait. The second winter, too, was more severe and stormy than the first.

December came in with one of those tremendous snowstorms which are perhaps the most frightful visitations of polar regions. All the *Investigators* could do was to remain shut up in the ship, and wonder what the animals of Banks Land did in a snowdrift [blizzard] which almost tore the housing from its many fastenings. A solid moving body of snow rolled along higher than the topmast heads, and when it met the impediment of the ship, formed a wreath to windward, and became piled over her, until the weight of the accumulated snow broke down the floe in which the ship was frozen; the inclination of the ship first one way, then another, and the report made by the cracking of the ice under her bottom, startled to those unaccustomed to such accidents.

Reduced rations made one and all less fit to withstand these hard conditions; but in one respect they were better off than in the season before. The ship was only a few hundred yards from the shore, and the rocky coast was, as they soon found, backed by broad plains dotted with dwarf willows, where reindeer moss and the coarse grasses of the North supported surprising numbers of musk-oxen, caribou, and hares. In the deep night of midwinter no one had ventured far from the ship; but in the growing light of February hunting was carried on vigorously by a number of the crew, among whom Miertsching, Sergeant Woon of the Marines, and the boatswain were the most active.

The boatswain had made a most unpromising début as a hunter at Ballast Beach a few months before. After firing one shot at a musk-ox, he poured a second charge down the barrel, and rested his chest on the muzzle while he groped in his pouch for a bullet. The powder in the barrel exploded, burning his clothing and scorching his stomach. The poor man was assisted to the ship in a state of great alarm and discomfort, and could scarcely be persuaded by the surgeon that he was not mortally wounded. This incident caused great mirth to his shipmates, who suggested that a marlin-spike was the only proper weapon for a boatswain to use when he went hunting. In this time of necessity, however, he proved one of the most perservering and successful of the ship's providers.

Sergeant Woon distinguished himself in a manner even more honourable. There was in the ship's company a negro, Anderson, "who represented himself as a Canadian"—a fugitive, no doubt, from one of the slave states to the south. This man on one occasion strayed from his comrades when in pursuit of a deer, and was overtaken by darkness and fog. Panic-striken and exhausted, he had sunk down in the snow when the sergeant came upon him and persuaded him to get up and make an effort to save himself. He soon collapsed again, bleeding at the mouth and nose, and partially convulsed, Anderson was the heaviest man on board, Woon one of the lightest; but to leave him where he was, if only for an hour, meant death by freezing, even if he escaped the wolves, which were forever on the prowl.

So the sergeant slung both guns over his shoulder—like the good soldier that he was, he took care of equipment—and stooping down, he grasped his disabled comrade by the armpits, and in this awkward and exhausting posture dragged him for miles towards the ship. Reaching the top of a hill, he tumbled his burden down it, and so aroused him partially from the deadly drowsiness that was coming over him. Within a mile of the ship they were met by a rescue party and quickly conveyed to warmth and safety. Anderson underwent amputation of toes, fingers, and part of the nose. "A zealous hunter," says Armstrong, "could always be recognized by his disfigured face—the result of frequent frost-bites."

18 February
A snowstorm, of which no one in our country could form any conception, has lasted without a break for a week, and has so buried the ship that only the masts are visible at the top of an enormous white mass. We groan at being restained from hunting; for the chase is doubly precious to our appetites, which are always craving and never satisfied. Yesterday's hunger simply seems to add itself to the hunger of today.

One day our best hunters got three caribou. They came back to obtain transport from the ship, and delighted us with the good news. When they returned with a sledge they found that the wolves had laid thievish hands on the prey. We could have wept.

The wolves were a constant nuisance. They made it impossible to leave a carcass unguarded, carried off wounded animals that might otherwise have been bagged by the hunter, and aroused the enmity of the whole crew by a bold attempt to cut off the ship's mascot, an Eskimo dog. Neither force nor trickery prevailed against these pests; they were too wary to be shot, and avoided all traps set for them. Only two were killed, and that in the next winter, just before the desertion of the ship.

Though the wolves generally kept their distance, Mr. Kennedy, the boatswain, once had a close encounter with them. One evening he shot at and broke two legs of a buck but, as darkness was coming, he returned to the ship without securing his prey, and set out cheerfully the next morning to bring in the venison. On arriving at the spot he found to his disgust that five wolves were ahead of him. He advanced on them, calling them "all the names that a boatswain could think of".

The shameless creatures backed away a few feet only, with so savage an aspect that he dared not shoot one of them with his single-barrelled gun, "for fear of the rest doing as much to him as they had done to the buck". So he picked up a dismembered limb and tucked it under his arm, and tried to drag off the rest of the half-picked carcass by one end, while a she-wolf tugged at the other.

The wolves were snarling savagely, and the boatswain was shouting for help, when Miertsching, attracted by the uproar, came running over a hill, and was half frightened and half amused at the sight of the usually self-important and pompous petty officer in a frantic tussle with a wolf, "the female of the species", for a tattered remnant of deer's meat. So close together were they in their tug of war that for a moment he thought that Kennedy himself was being attacked.

The wolves slunk further off at Miertsching's approach, but followed the two men at a distance and kept them under observation until Dr. Armstrong came in sight; then they gave up and trotted away. They had much the best of the deal; Mr. Kennedy brought back twenty pounds of meat instead of the hundred and twenty which he had promised his mates.

It was soon found wise to make regulations for hunting: "It is to be a monopoly of those who are good shots; the others, who do nothing but frighten the game, are to abstain." A sensible rule, no doubt; but the licensed hunters were too few, and for that matter, the game too scarce, for them to find food for a company of sixty-six. Health and energy declined, and a spirit of weariness and indifference spread through the ship as the long winter drew to a close. On March 28th Miertsching notes:

> The sailors' school closed yesterday for want of scholars. Is must be admitted that when one is poorly fed, and has wandered all day on snow and ice, he is not in the frame of mind, when evening comes, to devote himself to study. It is more agreeable to smoke a pipe of tobacco, and chat about the events of the day.

The monotony of the station was relieved by the presence of one type of friendly animal life.

> Two ravens established themselves as friends of the family in Mercy Bay, living mainly by what little scraps the men might have to throw away after mealtimes. The ship's dog, however, looked upon these as his special perquisites, and exhibited considerable energy in maintaining his rights against the ravens, who nevertheless outwitted him in a way which amused everyone. Observing that he appeared quite willing to make a mouthful of their own sable persons, they used to throw themselves intentionally in his way just as the mess-tins were being cleaned out on the dirt-heap outside the ship. The dog would immediately run at them, and they would just fly a few yards; the dog made another run, and again they would appear to escape him but by an inch, and so on

until they had tempted and provoked him to the shore, a considerable distance off. Then the ravens would make a direct flight to the ship, and had generally made good execution before the mortified-looking dog detected the imposition that had been practised upon him, and rushed back again.

In the previous autumn, when the battered *Investigator* with her exhausted crew had dragged herself around Cape Providence into the Bay of Mercy, her captain had had little thought but for bare survival. But in the quiet days that followed other anxieties began to trouble him. The harbour that he had so gratefully entered was a deep inlet, undisturbed by ocean current or strong tide. It froze thick and firm. Only a strong summer gale from the south could drive out the ice and give his ship release. McClure noted with uneasiness that the prevailing winds were from the north, and the fear came upon him that the open water he had found was an unusual accident, and that the harbour might remain frozen and his ship a prisoner for years before the ice went out again. Sir John Ross had, he knew, been thus imprisoned in Regent's Inlet for two summers; and he was too deep in the ice to make his escape by sledge and boat as Ross had done. He heard his officers muttering that the Bay of Mercy was well named, for it would have been a mercy if they had never entered it.

In this difficulty he rested his hopes upon the four ships of Captain Horatio Austin. It had been that officer's intention to come as far west as Melville Island; his squadron might even now be berthed in Winter Harbour, just across the sound. Had he come and gone he would certainly have left a cache of provisions for the benefit of the Franklin castaways. The *Investigators* could use these to tide themselves over another winter, if they could not break out that season. So on April 11, 1852, McClure set out across Melville Sound with a sledge crew and his trustiest officer, Mr. Stephen Court.

The first stage of the outward journey was made difficult by wind and fog. The ice was so rough that when they lost their way and strayed back on to the rock-strewn coast, they did not at first realize that they were on land. Later they came upon smooth ice of one year's growth, which proved the truth of Mr. Court's report that the sea had been open the autumn before. They reached the shore of Melville Island, and on the eighteenth day rounded Cape Hearne and entered the bay at the bottom of which lay Parry's old base of Winter Harbour. One can imagine with what a searching gaze they scanned the shore as its outline grew clearer, looking in vain for the housed-in, snow-covered hulks that would be a sign that they were not deserted and forgotten. The smooth expanse of the sea-ice was unbroken, and as they drew nearer they saw that no trace of food-cache or cairn interrupted the level line of the beach.

Cruelly disappointed, the travellers approached the mass of sandstone that stood a little back from the shore—Parry's monument on the front of which were carved the names of the ships, *Hecla* and *Griper,* and of their captains, W. E. Parry and M. Liddon. Their curiosity was excited by a pile of stones on the top of the monument; these were brushed off, and a small metal cylinder fell to the ground. What was it? Notice of Franklin? They waited with bated breath while McClure opened the tube. Alas, no. The paper inside was dated only ten months before and signed F. L. McClintock.

From it they learned that owing to ice Austin had not been able to get his ships within two hundred miles of Melville Island, and that McClintock had made the journey with one sledge only. Had McClure only sent a party over from Princess Royal Islands the spring before, McClintock and Austin would have had notice of his whereabouts. Where was Austin now? Searching elsewhere, or returned to England? It would have been better for McClure to find no record at all than one that destroyed his hopes so pitilessly. The disheartened travellers carried the news back to the ship. "I see that our poor captain makes a great effort to keep a cheerful face, and not to yield to discouragement," wrote Miertsching.

Chapter ten

Summer brings no release.

McCLURE DID not suspect that he was very close to
a comrade ship, nor that a few days after his return from Winter
Harbour his tracks had been crossed by a sledge crew of the
Enterprise. In the autumn of 1850 Collinson had arrived at
Bering Strait, too late to make his way through; he went south to
winter at Hong Kong. More fortunate the next summer, he had
followed the course of the *Investigator* along the Canadian north
shore, up to Nelson Head, and entered Prince of Wales Strait
a few days after the *Investigator* quitted it.

At the top of the strait he found himself, like McClure, stopped
by "immense fields of ice". He found a cairn that reported the
Investigator's movements up to that point, so put about and began
to follow that ship around the Banks Land shore. In the days
when the *Investigator* was nearly wrecked at Ballast Beach, the
Enterprise was only a few hours' sail behind her. But Collinson,
though a brave and capable navigator—the best, according to the
Norwegian Amundsen, that Great Britain ever sent in to the
Arctic—was too prudent to put his ship into the polar pack as
McClure had done. He sheered off from the heavy ice, and sailed
back to winter at the south end of Prince of Wales Strait.

With a better sense than McClure of what the situation required, he took the first opportunity with the return of spring of
sending Lieutenant Parkes up the strait, with orders to cross the
sound and plant a record at Winter Harbour. Sickness among his
men prevented Parkes from quite finishing the journey: he saw
McClure's tracks, but supposed that they were made by Eskimos.
And so the *Investigator* was left isolated.

It did not matter greatly. Collinson's resources were not

much larger than McClure's; and though for three winters he kept his crew healthy and cheerful in the most brilliant manner, he would have been sadly embarrassed by the need of helping Mc-Clure from the dangerous position in which he had placed himself.

Miertsching's journal for the summer of 1852 continues:

31 May

The health of the crew is beginning to alter perceptibly. Lack of nourishment and low spirits are the chief causes. A dense fog sometimes overtakes our hunters. Finger-posts pointing to the ship have been set up in all directions.

20 June

Here we are in the days when the sun never sets. The snow is dazzling white. Despite green glasses, fourteen men are suffering from the snow-blindness characteristic of this region. It has been forbidden to hunt except during those hours which correspond to night in more southerly latitudes, and during which the sun is less powerful. After a fresh examination of provisions it is found necessary to throw away several quarters of tainted meat. Our sailors look at them with a sigh. Now that we are on half-rations, we can survive until August of next year.

We have no fewer than a dozen sick.

30 June

On an excursion we find ruins of dwellings and stones arranged in circles after the custom of the Eskimos where they wish to raise a tent. Everywhere indeed where we have been able to explore this land of Banks or Baring, which we have been coasting around for two years, we have found the same phenomena. It was well peopled once.

9 July

The temperature is mild. No sooner has the snow disappeared than a multitude of little flowers, yellow and blue, appear on the moss. I have already gathered more than three thousand varieties of plants, mosses, and lichens. Orders are that the hunters are not to appropriate the game that they capture, but turn it over to the quartermaster for distribution. Their sole privilege is to claim a particular cut. Certain animals, not considered game—the fox, for instance—become the exclusive property of the man who kills them.

Sergeant Woon had gone out yesterday for the hunt in which he usually has good luck, when, beyond the mountain, he found himself face to face with two musk-oxen. Although he had only three bullets, he attacked them boldly. The wounded animals pursued him. In this emergency he was obliged to load his weapon first with the screw of his ramrod, and then with the ramrod itself. Finally he remained master of the battlefield. Much excited he came to report his victory. We received him with a roll of drums. Certainly for a starving group such as we, six hundred and forty seven pounds of beef are not to be despised. The two animals weigh together twelve hundred and fifty pounds undressed.

17 July

I take my walks during the hours of night. Yesterday I heard with delight the murmur of a little spring which until now the ice had held prisoner. I thought that never had poet enjoyed more the sound of wave or of wind in the leaves than did I the ripple of this brook splashing gently against the ice of its banks in the heart of this desolate landscape.

We are in midsummer. Here that means the season of sudden showers and cloudbursts. The cloudbursts are sudden squalls of snow which envelop our hunters.

I have caught some pretty butterflies. They are of almost the same species as are found in Labrador.

Dr. Armstrong, like Miertsching, was abroad in the summer months making notes on plant and animal life. He marvelled at the rich loam in the ravines and valleys, which in a few weeks produced an abundance of vegetation, and attracted the musk-ox and caribou but for which the explorers must have utterly starved. Banks Land, he found, was not at all the harsh and barren country that he had supposed on seeing it in winter or viewing it at a distance from the deck of a ship. He found many interesting fossils, and made a journey to confirm Lieutenant Cresswell's report of coal formations in the sandstone. To do this he had to wade deep in water and melting snow, and came back rather wishing that he had taken Mr. Cresswell's word for it.

The frozen sea responded much more slowly than the land to the warmth of summer, and through June and early July the imprisoned men curbed their impatience, knowing that it was too early to hope for release. They continued to hunt, but without much success, for the caribou and musk-oxen had moved inland at that season.

One of the men had a close encounter with game of a different kind. William Whitefield, the man who had so nearly perished in a blizzard the year before, had wandered along the ice to the entrance of the bay, when he suddenly found himself within twenty feet of a polar bear. He had the presence of mind not to run, nor to irritate the bear by a wound that might not be fatal; he brought his gun to his shoulder and tried to stare the animal out. They were facing each other when another bear appeared and came briskly up to within forty yards. So the three stood for several minutes, when to Whitefield's inexpressible relief the two bears turned and shambled off. As soon as it seemed safe the carpenter ran off as fast as he could, rejoicing at his escape. Polar bears had always fled from *parties* of men; Whitefield was the first to test their response to one man alone.

About the middle of July a slowly broadening margin of water appeared along the shore of the bay, and some asserted that out to sea the ice was in motion, though no open water was visible. Restlessness could be kept down no longer. Wrote Miertsching:

Each day some or others of us climb the mountain,

eight hundred feet high, to see if there is the least sign of movement in the ice of the open sea. Up till now there is not a trace. The will of God be done! "All things work together for good to them that love Him."

I made a real find today. It is a kind of sorrel, growing in abundance on a southern slope. I washed it and brought it to dinner as a surprise—a fresh salad! The doctor applauded me, and said that my greens were an excellent preventive of scurvy.

On August 10th the lookout joyfully reported that the sea ice was in motion, and traces of water visible. But the bay ice remained as immovable as the cliffs that surrounded it, and it was noticed with uneasiness that northerly winds blowing off the sound were driving the broken ice in shore and fencing the bay in with a growing barrier of hummocks. It was also found that the bay contained numerous shoals that retarded the outward movement of the ice. "It required, therefore," says Armstrong, "a combination of the most favourable circumstances to free it." More than ever the captive sailors realized that the ice-free water that had enticed them into that treacherous haven, did not occur every year.

The northerly winds continued to blow; the sun was fast receding, and at night ice was forming on the pools. "Nothing new at sea," writes Miertsching for August 16th:

> Melancholy is overcoming our most determined optimists. The sea is open for a width of about fifteen paces along the beach, which obliges us to make constant use of the rubber boat. This boat, ten feet by three, carries ten men and weighs only twenty-five pounds. One of us takes it under his arm, and on arriving at the water's edge, inflates it with a pocket pump. It is the handiest of inventions!"

21 August

Our situation is only getting worse. Without doubt we had all given up hope of seeing our homes this year, but we had thought that we might at least reach Melville Island. Not only has the sea failed to open in response to our prayers, but new ice is forming, and has already attained a thickness of three inches.

To add to our troubles, a young sailor has gone mad. He has to be kept under guard by day; at night his heart-rending cries trouble the spirit. And, nevertheless, I would be a thankless creature if, on this anniversary of my birth, I did not render thanks to God with all my heart. Is it not He Who has blessed my feeble efforts on behalf of my comrades? Several are now bound together by a common faith. We join in happiness around His Word. We pray; we receive together the strength to support the burden of the day.

The health of the crew has been noticeably improved by the use of the sorrel of Banks Land.

On the 9th of September McClure declared that he had given up all hope of freeing the ship:

The captain assembled the crew today. In a firm voice he told them that he was giving up all hope of leaving the Bay of Mercy that year, and that they must prepare to spend another winter there. "Let us commit ourselves to God," he added; "He has never failed us. Behave like British seamen who know the meaning of courage and endurance. I feel sure that all of us to the last man will live to see our native land again."

He then regretfully told us of a step which he thought absolutely necessary: it was a further reduction in rations to ensure a supply for the summer of 1853, and also to make it possible to step up the allowance of food when the service demanded exertion.

The gathering broke up in silence with bowed heads, the persistent grumblers like the rest; for, after all, what objection *could* be made to the captain's action?

2 October

Here we are in the midst of winter with a long and melancholy prospect ahead of us. The loneliness of this place is oppressive. It is now some weeks since the birds with their twittering and their lively flight have been here to cheer us. They have all migrated to the south. Those of us who are not sustained by faith in God and in the assurance of His love are growing gloomy and peevish. They cannot bear up against this perpetual hunger. We can no longer gather lichens and wild sorrel, which had been a precious addition to our rations. All that is buried deep in snow.

Nothing is now the hunter's property. Everything must be turned in to the quartermaster. But sometimes the order is not obeyed; ptarmigan and hares have been devoured raw in concealment behind some rock.

Miertsching here makes an observation the truth of which was not fully appreciated many years later. "There is," he says, "in the regulations which govern us, as in all fixed rules, a great injustice: the quantity of food which is more or less enough for some leaves to others all the torments of famine."

Polar travellers were slow to grasp the weight of this sensible and fairly obvious remark, and one great disaster resulted from their neglect. Sixty years after Miertsching wrote these words, Captain Robert Falcon Scott and four devoted companions, dragging their heavy sledge, toiled up the steep and rugged ramp of the Beardmore Glacier on to the Antarctic plateau, and so forward many days' journey to the South Pole. There they found that Amundsen, travelling another route with dog sledges, was four weeks ahead of them.

On the journey back, one by one Scott's companions began to weaken and lag. The stronger men shortened their journeys rather than desert their failing comrades, and not one of the five came out alive from the wilderness of ice and snow that they had entered so hopefully. The captain and two others were found in their tent, a hundred and fifty miles from the base, frozen to death. In his journal Scott had recorded with surprise that the first man to fail had been Evans, "a tower of strength," the largest and strongest man of the party. The injustice of the fixed ration was the cause; the biggest frame had been the first to suffer want.

Miertsching was not the worst of the sufferers, but he was full of sympathy for those who were:

> Nothing has given me a keener impression of our distress than to see this morning some of the men groping eagerly in the heap of sweepings and garbage which have accumulated near the ship during our stay.

> 6 October
> To the pains of rheumatism, a disagreeable acquaintance which I made during our first winter, there has been added, in the last day or two, a stubborn toothache. One would so like to be warm when one has the toothache! I am chilled all day, and at night must retire to a bed that is quite damp. Lord, give me strength not to complain.

If Miertsching did not complain openly, there were others who did. "Today," he writes for October 18th,

> we had a small popular assembly. The sailors gathered on the deck without permission, held a meeting with a certain orderliness and restraint. Then, when the captain appeared, four of them approached him as spokesmen: "We respectfully request you, sir, to increase our rations a little. We can no longer endure it. We are sleepless with hunger."

> The captain replied mildly, and showed sympathy with their sufferings. He pardoned their unlawful assembly, and then tried to convince them that his regulations had been prescribed by absolute necessity, and that prudence demanded their continuance. But a starving

belly has no ears. Without departing from their respectful manner the sailors insisted, and the captain found himself obliged to grant a small increase.

It must have been a *very* small increase; Armstrong, who also describes the incident, mentions no change in rations at all. They were a very fine crew, as McClure himself was the first to admit, to be so orderly and reasonable when tortured by perpetual hunger.

26 October

For the anniversary of his discovery Captain McClure authorized the quartermaster to give us a full meal as in the days of abundance. The gaiety during the banquet, which was actually a very simple affair, shows how much our moral being is influenced by our physical wants. Expressions on faces were completely altered.

With all his narrowness on some points, Miertsching was a man of wide sympathies, for he adds:

Ah! experience is a great teacher. I do not think that hereafter any of us will be disposed to cast a stone at the beggar, who, in the midst of his want, seizes the opportunity to gorge himself to disgusting excess. One must have lived his life to understand his reaction.

But anniversaries come only once a year, and in the hungry days that followed the anxious castaways could sense the shadow of tragedy drawing nearer and nearer.

Our poor officer, Wyniatt, has been insane for some weeks. Except for his servant, I am the only one who can control him in the least without brute force. But his continual cries are a torture to the nerves; sometimes I have to flee the ship despite weather in which, as the saying goes, one would not put a dog out of doors. However far I go I seem to hear his voice pursuing me through the howling of the wind. Poor, poor fellow!

23 November

Happily we are not short of fuel. A blazing fire is continually kept going in the great stove, and there the cannon-balls are heated to be placed in our cabins. But for these I am convinced that we would die of cold and dampness. To pass the time officers and men knit and do trivial things which require little light.

30 November

Forty-two below. I was out hunting yesterday. I killed a hare, two ptarmigan, and a caribou. The ptarmigan and hare were straightway set aside for the sick.

The little food they had could not always be served in an appetizing manner:

This is how we have to take our beans this year. They are broken with a hammer, and then ground in an old coffee-mill; with water they are made into a paste, and then cooked in a serviette like a pudding. They are not succulent, certainly; but are, at least, something to eat. The quartermaster makes portions as equal as possible of everything that goes on the table; if any complaint is made, the men draw lots for the portions.

We have thirteen on the sick-list, all suffering from scurvy. [This glib diagnosis would have made Dr. Armstrong furious.]

6 December

Yesterday chasing a hare which I would have been delighted to bring to the sick-bay, I fell into a deep crevasse, from which I barely managed to climb out. I got off with a sprained ankle. Farewell to hunting for a long time!

15 December

Thanks to God, here I am on my feet sooner than I had dared to hope. This morning I killed a hare and a male caribou with fine antlers. In consequence of being well frozen my face and hands have become extremely tender. . . . Except for the two whose minds are impaired there is not one on board who does not hail the approach of Christmas with rejoicing. On that day we are to have a full meal. Alas, poor we!

25 December

. . . The day began with worship. At noon the meal awaited with such impatience was served. The sailors had decorated the lower deck with streamers, verses, and crude drawings representing the events of our voyage. Each table had a respectable plum-pudding. Then the quartermaster, who had, without anyone's knowledge, preserved a large piece of musk-ox, put it on the table where it was greeted with unanimous applause. The sick received some special delicacies. The lower deck was lighted all day, a great treat, which was enjoyed by everyone.

Chapter eleven

Can we survive?

THE WINTER of 1852-53 was much the severest that the adventurous crew had experienced. The thermometer went down as low as –67, and the mean for January was –43. But the cold and starving wanderers found that this was not altogether a bad thing, for caribou and hares were driven by the extremely low temperatures from the level inland plains into the valleys along the coast, where they were within easier reach of the ship. In previous winters the hunters had stayed indoors during the season of deep arctic midnight for fear of losing their way. Now the more imminent danger of starvation kept them in the field in spite of darkness,

> moon and starlight alone [says Armstrong] enabling us faintly to discern the object of which we were in anxious and eager pursuit. No temperature, however low, detained us from the pursuit, if unaccompanied by wind; but the latter, even in a slight degree, proved unendurable. It was therefore a common circumstance to find a hunter so benumbed and helpless as to be barely able to reach the ship, and with an utterance so impaired as to render his speech difficult to be understood, until rest and warmth restored those powers of nature which cold and hunger had well-nigh exhausted. . . . The blood of the Deer that were killed was, at this time, eagerly drunk by the hunter as it flowed fresh and warm from the wound, for the vivifying and sustaining influence which it exercised; but as it froze on the face as it flowed, he presented a frightful spectacle as he came on board.

But it was a heart-breaking pursuit. To strengthen himself for the exertion of the chase, the hunter was obliged to eat the greater portion of his day's allowance before setting forth; and, if he came back unsuccessful, went without food for the rest of the twenty-four hours, and was thus in worse plight than the idle comrades for whom he had spent his labour in vain. For the most part the men declined a duty in which exertion was likely to be penalized in such a way. No one could be ordered to share in a duty where genuine goodwill and determination were necessary to success, so the burden of hunting fell largely on the officers and petty officers, who, in the huddled misery of the captive ship, where rank had lost most of its privileges, were still mindful of its responsibilities. They suffered not a little in the zealous discharge of their duty.

"On the 4th of December," relates Armstrong, "while in pursuit of Reindeer [caribou] at a temperature of 36 below zero, my gun burst in my hands when in the act of firing; shattering the stock, but fortunately injuring me but little. It resulted from my inability to send the ball 'home', having been severly frost-bitten in the act."

Miertsching's hands became so raw and tender from repeated frost-bites that he could not endure to carry his gun on a long tramp, so he employed sailors to do this for him, and as a reward allowed them to drink the blood of the kill, and to feed on the undigested mosses and lichens found in the first stomach. The unchewed cud of a deer does not seem very appetizing food to us; but that gallant officer, Lieutenant Hooper, who carried the search for Franklin into the wastes of eastern Siberia, assures us that it was a favourite dish with the hospitable natives who received him into their tents.

By these means a weekly average of two hundred pounds of fresh meat was obtained—three pounds per capita in a ship's company of sixty-six—quite insufficient to support men on half rations, when they needed to be especially well fed to withstand the cold. Armstrong, who had weighed the entire crew on January 1, 1852, repeated the examination on the next New Year's Day: he found an average loss in weight of thirty-five pounds per man. Fuel began to run low; dampness and discomfort became more pronounced in proportion as the men grew less able to resist them. Scurvy was spreading through the ship: "The sick-list was growing; all were feeble, depressed, with a dull haggard stare."

It was in this miserable condition that they had to withstand the cold of the severest winter they had known. "The very ship seemed to suffer from it; and bolts, treenails, and fastenings were heard to crack under the influence of frost and contraction."

11 January [1853]

I never remember having been so cold. The springs of gun-locks and door-latches are snapping one after another. The caribou, obeying their instinct in cold weather, are quitting the interior and gathering along the coast: we have killed four in the last few days. It is a valuable addition, but there are sixty-six to claim a share in it. Even the skins of these animals, after having been boiled a long time, cut into strips, and salted, become food.

25 January

My toothache is no better; I am running a temperature, and am much depressed. Our mental cases are no better. Their cries resound in a frightful manner in the long night. Yesterday a sailor, returning half-frozen, let himself slip, while descending to the lower deck. His arm broke like glass. All these distresses are a grievous burden to our poor captain. God help him—and help us all!

22 February

The sun has returned, but it is to shed light on a gloomy situation. Our men are reduced to a state of extreme weakness. The stronger are employing themselves in loading sledges with sand, and in spreading it so as to form a broad way in the direction of the open sea. As a dark surface aids in the melting of the ice they hope thus to accelerate the liberation of the ship. They work with more perseverance than faith, and one is disposed to shake his head in measuring with the eye that long grey road.

Miertsching might well shake his head: the ice was seven feet thick; the harbour mouth two miles away. It says more for the spirit than for the judgment of the men that they thus used up what little strength was left them.

The men of the *Investigator* were now in the critical situation, which as later became known, had been fatal to Franklin's beleaguered crews. They had withstood the siege of three arctic winters, and stayed by their ship until they no longer had the strength to quit her. Nevertheless McClure thought that an attempt at escape was preferable to the slow starvation that seemed the only alternative. Rations at the present rate of use would last until the summer of 1854; but the ship might remain imprisoned that summer, and it was ridiculous to suppose that men already so much reduced in strength could outlive the cold of another winter.

On the 3rd of March, 1853, he declared his intentions to the assembled crew. Half of them must quit the ship in six weeks' time; of these one part, under Lieutenant Haswell, would journey east to Port Leopold (on Somerset Island, five hundred miles away), where, according to McClintock's Winter Harbour record, they would find a boat cached, with food, clothing, and fuel. When the sea opened they would man the boat, and sail east in the hope of being picked up by one of the whaling ships that plied their trade in Regent's Inlet and Baffin Bay.

The other party, under Lieutenant Cresswell, was to go down Prince of Wales Strait to Princess Royal Islands, where McClure himself had left a boat and supplies. When the ice broke up, they would sail over to the Canadian shore, and try to reach one of the trading posts on the Mackenzie River.

He himself, with thirty of the strongest men, would remain and endeavour to get the ship out that summer. Failing in this, they would, in their turn, journey to Port Leopold to be picked up by the rescue ship that would, of course, be sent from England, when Haswell arrived with his report.

But who believed that Haswell would ever get there? "A look at us," wrote Miertsching, "our leaness, and our weakness, a look at the hundreds of miles we must travel through snow and ice harnessed to a loaded sledge—Ah! there is reason to despair. . . . This communication of the captain's, which was heard in dead silence, has troubled the minds of us all. Those who are to travel, appalled at the prospect of a long journey, envy those who are to remain. The latter are equally envious of the travellers."

Armstrong took the first opportunity of warning the captain privately that journeys so long meant death to the men who attempted them. McClure heard him out in depressed silence, without altering his purpose; it was as well that way as the other. He put the prospective sledge parties on full rations, and, as the armourer was sick, employed Miertsching, who knew something of blacksmithing, in the manufacture of mess-tins.

The officers took care not to spread discouragement by giving voice to their fears, while the men, cheered by a more generous ration, grew hopeful. Those who were to remain with the ship busied themselves writing letters for home while the travellers were packing up. Only the barest necessities could be carried on the sledges, so each man bundled up his belongings and turned them over to the captain against his receipt. "Our property will be given back to us in England—if both he and we ever get there."

> After dinner today the captain and I took a walk together and spoke with regret of our coming separation. "If you get to England," said he, taking me affectionately by the hand, "and if you hear no more of Captain McClure and his men, you may imagine that his body lies somewhere wrapped in the good fur coat which you were kind enough to give him. But be sure at the same time that to my dying moment my Saviour will have been

my only hope, and that I will have died in the firm belief that one day at His divine voice this poor body will emerge from the tomb."

Chapter twelve

Rescuers on the way

N OT THE least tragic feature of the hardships and anxieties suffered by the men of the *Investigator* during their last winter at Mercy Bay was that they were wholly unnecessary—the crew need not have starved themselves to save their food reserves. They were neither forgotten nor deserted. Under the skyline to the north-east, where the rugged pack was softened by distance into the level line of the horizon, lay two ships manned by the "bravest choice of dauntless spirits" whom their country had ever sent forth. Kellett and McClintock were to come to the rescue; and by a coincidence, on the very day (September 9, 1852) when McClure announced to his crew that another winter must be passed on short rations, two rescue ships were on the other side of the sound, sawing their way into a harbour a little to the east of Parry's Monument.

In the summer of 1851, when McClintock returned from Winter Harbour with his negative report and other searching parties were equally unsuccessful, Captain Austin had sailed out of Lancaster Sound and gone northward into the Sound of Alderman Jones. There his ships were roughly handled in the ice; one of his steam-tenders, the *Pioneer,* was nipped and pushed up the side of an iceberg, and only by a miracle slid back into the water without capsizing. Finding no trace of Franklin in that quarter, Austin pulled his ships out and returned to England to report his ill success.

In his opinion the quest was hopeless; to continue it was to waste money and to risk lives; but the public did not give up so easily. The ships were refitted to make a fresh attempt the next summer; Sir Edward Belcher took command in the *Assistance,*

Kellett, just returned from the Pacific, became his second-in-command in the *Resolute,* McClintock and Osborn were appointed captains of the steam-tenders *Intrepid* and *Pioneer* respectively. Lieutenant Osborn was both a good officer and a gifted writer. He wrote a book on his own arctic travels, besides editing Captain McClure's journal.

McClintock's unsuccessful journey to Winter Harbour was taken as proof that Franklin's men were not to be looked for in that region of the Arctic, so Sir Edward Belcher was ordered to take his entire squadron up Wellington Channel and to direct his search to the far north. It was a terribly critical moment for the men of the *Investigator* when these instructions were issued; had they not been altered, McClure and all his men must have perished on the ship or on the march.

But before Sir Edward sailed, Mr. Cresswell, father of the *Investigator's* second lieutenant, addressed a letter to the Admiralty in which he reminded them that both Collinson and McClure knew that it had been Captain Austin's intention to take his ships, if possible, to Melville Island; and that if they had been ice-bound in the Western Arctic, they would make for Winter Harbour (as both actually had done), in the hope of finding ships there, or at least a cache of supplies. The *Investigator* was already two years unreported; he therefore urged that part of the squadron should be sent to Melville Island with orders to make a search not for Franklin only, but also for McClure.

Mr. Cresswell's suggestion was adopted; it was now determined that Belcher and Osborn only should go up Wellington Channel, while Kellett and McClintock took the westerly route to Melville Island. To ensure the safety of the crews a fifth ship, the *North Star,* was added to the squadron, to be berthed somewhere on the fringe of the search area, and serve as a base and point of retreat, in case any of the searching ships met with disaster.

Few commanders have been more fortunate in their officers than was Kellett on this famous cruise. McClintock and Mecham were veteran and unwearied sledge travellers, who had served on two ardous expeditions, and were now coming back for a third.

His junior lieutenant, Bedford Pim, had proved his quality by a long winter journey in Alaska, seeking information from the Russian sealing-stations. Not less deserving was George Mc-Dougall, master of the *Resolute*. He was a self-made man, who had acquired the scientific training of the officer without giving up the beliefs and superstitions of the simple sailor class from which he sprang. He wrote a history of this voyage, confused and incoherent, but full of lively anecdotes.

They are all dead and gone for the best part of a hundred years, McDougall and his comrades; and their works have vanished with them. Today the old *Resolute* is as outmoded as Noah's Ark; the airplane skims in seconds over the distances which those plodding sledge travellers measured in weary hours; but they still live for us, with their sense of duty that knew no doubt or hesitation, with their comradeship, their cares, and their jests, in the pages of this honest diarist.

The expedition met with bad weather on the way out to Greenland, and the *Resolute,* deeply laden, as were all the discovery ships, was compelled to lie to in a gale, rolling much to the discomfort of her crew, and inspiring her master to spin one of the yarns in which he brings back to us the atmosphere of those bygone days:

> The *Shannon* of Hull, when outward bound, fell in with a gale of wind, about 200 miles N.W. of Cape Farewell. At midnight the ship was under snug sail, but the dark masses of heavy clouds, driving across a wild looking sky, cast a dense shadow on the heaving sea relieved only by the snowy crest of the toppling waves.
>
> The watch had just been relieved, when a fearful crash told the awful tale—the ship had struck a "washing piece"! The bows of the ill-fated ship were stove in instantaneously, and, horrible to relate, the men of the watch below, who had just lain down, were crushed to death by the ice whose progress was at length arrested by the foremast.

The men on deck rushed to the rigging, but the ship commenced filling; and falling over on her broadside, launched the men on that side of the rigging into eternity. Few only now survived, and they were in momentary expectation of the ship sinking; fortunately she did not (I can only attribute her not sinking to the buoyancy of the casks on board); but they remained in this fearful state of suspense for many days, and were obliged to have recourse to sucking their own and each other's blood to sustain life. They were eventually rescued by a Danish vessel, and landed at Elsinore, where my informant then was.

Strange to say the Captain of the Danish vessel had for several nights dreamt some dreadful catastrophe had befallen a ship, in a certain latitude and longitude, and this vision had such an effect on his mind, as to induce him to steer in the direction pointed out, although quite out of his course; which was usually along the coast, as they were accustomed to call at the settlements.

If the assigned cause for his altering course be true, the result proved the special intervention of Providence.

Though no such horrible fate befell the *Resolute* or any of her comrade ships, they had a difficult passage up to the top of Baffin Bay, and *en route* saw two whalers nipped and sunk. As it was early in the season and they were in no hurry, they also called at various settlements to pay courtesy visits to Danish officials and obtain Eskimo dogs and sledges. On one of the whale-fishing islands McDougall found the following curious epitaph marking the grave of a British whaler:

> *You mariners that pass by here,*
> *Upon my grave let fall a tear;*
> *Henry Markinson is my name;*
> *In the 'Albion', Captain Hill, I came:*
> *'Twas the month of April I came here,*

But did not think death was so near.
On the 15th day of April
It was my lot to have a fall.
From the cross-trees of the main-topmast,
I on the quarter-deck was cast,
And was so hurted by the fall,
My life soon after God did call.

Whatever we think of the quality of the verse, we can only admire the goodwill and industry of the composer, who carved these lines in a hardwood slab with such pains that in spite of weathering and decay they were legible thirty years after to the eye of the Irish sailor who transcribed them.

Godhavn on the island of Disco was a favourite port of call for the British discovery ships, for there they had their last taste of human companionship. The *Resolute* had not been long at anchor here when a boatload of Danish and Eskimo girls came off and joined in a dance on the quarter-deck, where they made such an uproar that officers came over from the other ships to join in the fun. Two of these girls, who McDougall notes as being the prettiest, were seven years later to be the first Europeans to greet the toil-worn McClintock when he brought out the only written record of Franklin's fate that has ever come to light.

This visit was returned the following day:

> In the evening we held a little fête at the house of the fair Sophy. The room was perhaps fifteen feet square, and in it were congregated about thirty persons, the majority of whose garments were made of seal, or deer skin; this fact, and I say it with all due deference to the wearers, who were principally ladies, was not conducive to our comfort; we were therefore obliged to have recourse to the open air, where we danced until near midnight, and then, quite worn out with fatigue, repaired on board.

Thirty persons dancing in a room fifteen feet square, probably with a low-pitched ceiling, and the majority wearing in June the clothing that is nature's device for warding off the cold of January! No wonder that "with all due deference" to the ladies someone was bold enough to suggest moving outside!

Quitting Godhavn, the little squadron stretched to the north and then to the west into Lancaster Sound. The ships became scattered in fog, but in early August all rendezvoused safe and undamaged at Beechey Island, where the *North Star* was ordered to make her berth. Sir Edward Belcher with the *Assistance* and *Pioneer* went up Wellington Channel, while the *Resolute* and *Intrepid* took the westerly course through Barrow Strait, which, though they did not suspect it, was bringing them daily nearer the starving men of the *Investigator*.

Barrow Strait proved to be badly choked up, and though the ice had not nearly the weight and depth of the polar pack of Beaufort Sea, it was several feet thick, and the *Resolute* experienced the same danger, though in lesser degree, that McClure had encountered the autumn before in his voyage up the west shore of Banks Land. She had to weave her way between land and the floating pack, with frequent risk of running aground or being pushed ashore by the ice. On one occasion she found herself in suddenly shoaling water; she tried to put about, but took the ground on a submerged ridge of stone and gravel. The tide was at its peak; there was no hope of its rising higher to give the stranded vessel a lift. So boats were hoisted out and the deck cargo transferred to the *Intrepid,* which lay afloat a cable's length away. In the meantime the tide was receding, and the ship began to lie over at an angle of twenty degrees.

There was nothing for the men of the *Resolute* to do but to await with patience the return of the tide; but in the meantime their attention was drawn to a new and horrifying sight. A little distance ahead of them lay what they had supposed to be a low ice-sheathed cape. The startled crew now perceived this to be in motion; it was no sand-spit, but an ocean floe, which was pivoting on its landfast end and swinging in shore directly towards them. "No power of ours could either stop its progress or hinder its course." McClintock in the *Intrepid* started his engines and steamed out of the narrowing corridor before it was too late. The *Resolute* lay perched on her gravel ridge, a sitting duck.

> About seven the edge of the ice took the ship under the lee gangway, shaking her throughout. A moment had scarcely elapsed ere we became sensible of the ship's lifting, and instinctively each man grasped a rope, as he became aware that she would inevitably be thrown over. Yielding inch by inch before such a powerful lever, the ship at length rested on her keel, but it was but momentary, for in a second she was thrown over on her starboard side with a shock sufficient to bring every mast by the board.
>
> As it was, the very topmasts bent like whalebone, bringing a fearful strain on the weather shrouds; but not a rope was stranded, not a single spar injured by this unprecedented occurence. [The discoverers always spoke well of the work done at the Chatham shipyards.]

Had the pressure continued undiminished, the ship would have been either crushed or driven up the bank beyond the power of man to refloat her; but luckily the shoal bottom arrested the advance of the ice. With this fear removed, the *Resolutes* eagerly scanned the surface of the channel for a glimpse of their consort. A thin wreath of smoke drifting over the ice drew their eyes to the masts and smoke-stack of the *Intrepid,* safely hove to on the seaward edge of the floe. Several anxious hours followed; then the ice was perceived to be moving off shore and to the east. The *Intrepid* came into clear view, rounding the western end of the floe and returning to the station she had so hurriedly quitted. A hawser was carried out to her and she succeeded in tugging the *Resolute* off the bank into deep water.

The forlorn *Investigators,* marooned far away among ice and rocks, did not dream that that afternoon they had had the narrowest of their many narrow escapes. A crippling accident to the *Resolute* would have been fatal to them.

Though this near-disaster was not repeated, the navigation was so difficult that Kellett spent six weeks in covering the two hundred and fifty miles to Winter Harbour, which he had chosen as a berth for the winter and a base for the sledge journeys of the next spring. Rugged in many places, Melville Island is flat thereabouts; and a fresh-fallen snow made it difficult to tell where the harbour lay. Even McClintock, the only officer to have visited the place, was puzzled until clear weather and a bright sun melted the snow from Parry's Monument and brought it into dark relief against the flat and whitened landscape around it. Then they saw that six miles of tightly packed ice lay between them and the desired anchorage. No possible harbour here. Kellett wasted no time in visiting the Monument; McClintock had done so the year before and found it empty. Autumn was fast advancing, and an icy sludge was forming on the sea. So the two ships put about to the east, and sawed and blasted their way into a safe anchorage between the shore of Melville Island and an islet named Dealy. McClure's records were left undiscovered on the top of the sandstone rock.

As soon as the ships were secured McClintock and Mecham set out with carts and sledges, the one to the north and the other to the west, to establish food depots for their use on the long journeys of discovery planned for the spring. Mecham spent a month in placing stores on Liddon Gulf. His return was marked by the most surprising and dramatic happening in the history of the Canadian Arctic. His party was coming home, tired but relaxed, drawing empty sledges and trundling along with the unloaded cart, a little inland from Winter Harbour.

It occurred to the foot-sore Mecham that he ought to do what in their haste to secure the ships had previously been omitted, and pay a visit to the sandstone rock. So he trudged down to the beach, pulled the stones down from the top of the Monument and picked up the well-known cylinder, merely intending to add a note of his visit to the record of McClintock. On opening the cylinder, he found to his utter astonishment that he held in his hand not the slip of paper left there by his shipmate on the former expedition, but the chart of H.M.S. *Investigator's* cruise and McClure's journal of proceedings.

In a moment he knew that the Northwest Passage had been found two years before, and he was the first outsider to know it. With growing excitement he realized that the men who had achieved this glorious feat were in trouble and might even at that moment be lying ice-bound near at hand just across the sound, sorely in need of help. He hurried back to the sledges and urged on his lagging crew to make all haste to the ship with the news.

Chapter thirteen

Will they come in time?

O N RECEIVING this surprising intelligence, Kellett called
his officers to a council of war. They were all of the opinion
that the *Investigator* was still at Banks Land; McClure's journal
stated his intention, if he got free, of coming out by Parry's route
along the north shore of Barrow Strait. Had he done so, in the
unending daylight of summer he must have been sighted going
out by the *Resolute* and *Intrepid* coming in. Therefore it seemed
most likely that he was ice-bound for a second winter.

None the less, Kellett regretfully came to the decision that no
attempt to communicate with him could be made until spring.
The latitude and longitude of Mercy Bay, as given by McClure,
placed it a hundred and sixty miles away. The north winds of
that summer, which had packed the ice against the Banks Land
shore, had left great stretches of open water on the north shore
of the sound. By the time these were safely frozen winter and
perpetual darkness would be upon them.

After all, McClure *might* have got out that summer and been
carried away to the west. In that case an autumn rescue party
would not only make a difficult journey to no purpose, but would
be obliged to come straight back to Dealy Island—a round trip
of over three hundred miles. So the *Investigators* were left to
spend their third winter in hunger and loneliness, not suspecting
that abundant supplies, and a hundred comrades eager to help,
lay just over the skyline to the north-east.

For Kellett's men the winter was one of cheerful activity. The
captain was a big, hearty Irishman, very different in disposition
from the shy and reserved McClure. He invited the crews to

form a theatre club, and was himself elected its principal director. To McDougall, the diarist, fell the tasks of scene-painting and costume designing. The forethought of the officers had provided some parts of ladies' attire before leaving England; the rest were improvised on board by the ship's carpenter. Stiff canvas was found to make excellent petticoats; the bustle was composed of a comforter stuffed with oakum, making what McDougall coyly calls the actresses' "after part" resemble "a miniature dome of St. Paul's".

The temperature on the stage was zero—"no joke in petticoats", McDougall, who played female parts, assures us; and the "actresses", when off stage, were obliged to arch their legs over a stove and swill hot whisky-punch. The performances were heartily enjoyed by all ranks; and the *Intrepid's* master, Mr. Krabbé, helped to pass the time by the feats of conjuring for which he was famous.

The routine of winter quarters was varied by the occasional chase after a polar bear. One of the men had a narrow escape from one of these creatures. He had descended to the ice to register the thermometers (for accuracy placed a short distance from the ship), and was intent on reading them when he heard a heavy breathing close behind him. Looking round, he saw a bear only five yards away. "One spring of the brute would have put an end to his registering thermometers forever." Luckily he had the presence of mind to throw the glare of his lamp full in the beast's eyes, and the startled animal turned round and shambled off.

Though Kellett had not authorized the autumn journey to the Bay of Mercy, he was very anxious about McClure and his men. With the coming of January, 1853, the *Investigator* had been three years at sea. Her supplies must be running low; and Kellett guessed, as was partly the case, that as soon as the weather moderated McClure would quit the ship and get his men out as best he could. Anxious to make contact before this happened, he thankfully accepted Lieutenant Pim's offer to make the earliest journey yet attempted, and set out at the beginning of March.

The cold was as severe and the winds as fierce as ever; but they had what they most desired—daylight.

Equipped with two sledges, one man-handled and the other drawn by dogs, with Dr. Domville as second in command, and nine men he left the ship on March 10th. For the first part of the journey his route lay along the shore of Melville Island, where the ice was smoother than on the open sea; but he was much hindered by blizzards, and when a few days out broke the large man-drawn sledge beyond repair. The malignant spirit that had twice nearly thwarted the efforts of the rescuers was still active.

It was a cruel position for Pim, a young lieutenant suddenly faced with a terrible responsibility. He dared not lose time by going back for help, for he had been warned that McClure might abandon ship by the 1st of April; yet he had lost most of his transport. He resolved to stake his chances on the unfamiliar and, he supposed, untrustworthy dogs; so he ordered Dr. Domville to make camp on the shore of Melville Island and await his return, and taking two men and the dog-sledge he quitted the land and plunged into the rugged pack of Melville Sound.

It was a hard trip for the three men so suddenly deprived of companionship and thrown on their own in strange and unfriendly surroundings. By day they were vexed with cruel winds; by night their eyes were burned and their faces fouled and blackened by the smoke of the native lamp that was their only source of heat. Others, by months of practice under Eskimo tuition, have learned to live the life of the Eskimo; these three brave fellows were flung into it without warning or preparation. They were learning to fight, not in an orderly training camp, but in the heat and uncertainty of the battle front itself. Afraid they certainly were, afraid of many things—but most of all of going back to report failure to the captain who had chosen them as the fittest men for the task.

So they went on without faltering, weaving in and out among the hummocks, now chopping a road with the ice-axe, now getting behind the sledge to heave it up the steep face of the ice, and then gently easing it down the opposite slope. If it escaped their grip, to slither sideways and crash on the frozen sea, there was an end to their journey, and perhaps to themselves. They did not know what they would find in the Bay of Mercy, and must have wondered whether the journey might not prove to be in vain; but as the days went by they were cheered by the sight of the sandstone cliffs of Banks Land rising higher and clearer to the south above that weary waste of ice.

Pim studied the shore-line through his telescope. That projecting point would, no doubt, be the Cape Back of McClure's chart, and the gap in the cliffs beyond it the Bay of Mercy; it must be—the map showed no other such bay between it and Cape Russell. Would they find the ship, manned or deserted? Would the poor fellows be found frozen to death, like Sir Hugh Willoughby's men in their Lapland harbour? They would soon know.

One morning Pim climbed up on a hummock and, raking the shore-line with his telescope, saw over the rough sea-ice into the snow-covered level of Mercy Bay. Suddenly he uttered a cry that startled the dogs and brought a shouted enquiry from the men. Past Cape Back, on the far side, the bay's smooth surface was heaved up into a low half-oval hump, where the drifted snow had swept level with the ship's upper deck. It was the *Investigator* all right; her masts were plainly visible, thin and upright above the housing. "But are they still alive, are they still there?" Pim steadied his foot, and again put the glass to his eye. Over the half-buried hulk he made out the faint stir of smoke and vapour. They had come in time!

In the years to come men were to spend years in learning the skills of the Eskimo and the habits of the seal, and, travelling with accurate, high-powered rifles and other modern equipment, to make winter journeys several times as long as that from Dealy Island to Mercy Bay. But those three men, Bedford Pim, Robert Hoyle, and Thomas Bidgood, were reared in country where winters of the Arctic kind were unknown; they were bred to the sea, not to travel on foot. They were placed in a situation where the timidity of inexperience was intensified by their ignorance of just what lay ahead. It is easy when one knows how. They did *not* know how, but they never flinched. They deserve to be remembered with the far more successful travellers who came after them.

Pim put his gun and telescope on the sledge, and, bidding the men come after him as fast as they could, he set off, scrambling over the high hummocks and vaulting over the low ones, running for all he was worth into Mercy Bay.

Chapter fourteen

The Investigator *deserted*

I N T H E meantime the *Investigators* had been going ahead
with preparations for departure. On April the 5th occurred the
first death of the expedition—from scurvy. It was, as Dr. Armstrong remarked, surprisingly lucky that sixty-six men, suffering
hardships so unusual, had kept their numbers undiminished for
over three years; but the death, when it came, cast a deeper
shadow of fear and uncertainty over the sixty-five who remained.

Feeling this, McClure, who always found it difficult to con-
verse with the men, called them together, and without attempting
to make light of the dangers that threatened both those who went
and those who remained, did his best to cheer and encourage
them all. He told them to keep pride in themselves and in the
service to which they belonged, and to meet the worst that befell
them with the courage of British seamen. He wound up with a
well-worn figure of speech: "Every cloud has its silver lining".

Seldom has a pep-talk been given in circumstances more de-
pressing, and seldom has it been more quickly and completely
justified. On the next morning McClure was walking near the
ship and discussing with the first lieutenant the preparations for
the funeral, when they noticed the figure of a man rapidly approaching from the rough ice at the entrance of the bay.

Three years of close companionship had taught McClure to
know every man on board. This figure resembled none of them;
but he might be one of the crew trying out a new travelling dress,
and, from his frantic haste, appeared to have been frightened
by a bear.

As he drew nearer they saw that his features were black as
ebony. He slackened his pace, made gesticulations, and uttered

a cry that, in the stir of the wind, "sounded like a wild screech". McClure called out: "In the name of God, who are you?" The stranger replied: "I'm Lieutenant Pim, late of the *Herald,* [forgetting his blackened features, Pim had expected to be recognized] now of the *Resolute.* Captain Kellett is in her at Dealy Island."

"To rush at and seize him by the hand was the first impulse, for the heart was too full to speak," wrote the grateful McClure. "The announcement of relief being close at hand, when none was supposed to be in the Arctic Circle, was too sudden, unexpected, and joyous for our minds to comprehend it at once."

Behind them a hum, a commotion, swelling up into a roar, told them that they had been observed from the ship. The cook quitted his kitchen, the artificers flung down their tools, the sick sprang from their beds to find out if the news was true. One hatchway only was opened, and the feebler men were sadly tumbled and jostled as one and all rushed to the deck and poured down the ramp on to the ice. "Despondency fled the ship, and Lieut. Pim received a welcome, pure, hearty, and grateful, that he will assuredly remember and cherish to the end of his days." "For a few hours," Miertsching drily informs us, "it seemed as if all our troubles were at an end and ourselves already at anchor in an English harbour." Longer trials lay ahead than even the level-headed German expected.

In a few minutes Pim's companions came up with the dog-sledge to share in the reception. When the first bustle of greeting was over they were much distressed at the halting gait, the lean, enfeebled frames, and the sunken, staring eyes of the *Investigator's crew.* The two seamen shed tears, while Pim ran to the sledge, and brought in a large parcel to give the ward-room mess the first bacon breakfast that had been theirs for many a month.

Pim then held a conference with the captain, the substance of which soon spread over the ship. He had brought a letter from Kellett, in which the latter, while generously praising McClure's exploit, and expressing the hope that the ship might be brought out, made it plain that, after their three years of hardship, he would not consent to any of the *Investigators* being compelled to prolong their term of service for the sake of the glorious but barren exploit of bringing their ship through the Northwest Passage. Every man must first be given a medical examination to test his fitness for continued service.

McClure was still resolved to save the *Investigator* and bring her home; but, if he demanded too much of his men, he cannot, at any rate, be accused of sparing himself. He was forty-six years old, and weakened by the same hard conditions that had broken down his crew. Yet he mustered a sledge party, and set out the very next day with Pim, to meet his superior officer and argue the question face to face. He gave in so far to Kellett's wishes as to leave orders that Lieutenant Cresswell and most of the men already appointed for travel should follow him in a few days to join the *Resolute* and go home with her.

The crew soon realized that, though the future was much more hopeful, the harsh realities of the present situation were unchanged. Two more deaths, occurring within a week, spread a new feeling of depression over the ship, and gave the men a superstitious eagerness to quit her before worse took place. Miertsching now found himself appointed, with Lieutenant Cresswell and the assistant surgeon, Mr. Piers, to take twenty of the feeblest men the hundred and sixty miles to Dealy Island. Of these, two were helpless or worse—one seaman in a state of idiocy, and Mr. Wyniatt violently insane. "Certainly it is a trying commission, but compared to the terrible journey we were about to undertake, anything is acceptable."

Miertsching, who had been as hard-working as a scientist as he had been as a diarist, was told that all his belongings must be left behind, and—if the ship was deserted, as appeared only too likely—be lost for good.

> We are preparing anew for departure; but no more than on the intended journey to the Mackenzie River are we allowed to carry more than is absolutely necessary. My geological specimens, my dried plants, my utensils and Eskimo weapons, have all been carefully stored on

the ship. I had hoped to obtain at least my manuscripts, but the captain's orders were rigid.

15 April

We are going to quit forever the ship which has carried us through calm and tempest, through good and evil fortune. I could not share the indifference of my comrades. For me the departure had a strange touch of sadness.

We dined together on full rations. At 2 P.M. I was for the last time united in the presence of God with those who, growing concerned over the welfare of their souls, had become my little flock. During the last half-hour before departure I received several visits which were very comforting to me. A young sailor, among others, who had at first been conspicuous by his ill-conduct, had become a beloved son to me. He had profited much from our night-school, writing easily and reading a great deal. We parted with emotion.

However, the hour had struck. We harnessed ourselves to the sledges, and after the resounding "hurrah" with which they saluted us from the ship, we set out. Lieutenant Cresswell walked in front, and with him the six men who were incapable of dragging anything but their poor suffering bodies. We travelled in this order for four hours and pitched our tents for the night at the extremity of a sandy cape.

16 April

After seven hours' rest the cold forced us to start moving at an earlier hour than we had intended. It had been a trying day. Our men have been so weakened by scurvy! Sometimes we come to blocks of ice heaved up by pressure to form regular steep mountains, and have to climb over these on our hands and knees, dragging the sledges after us as best we can. I could have yielded to despair had I not thought of One on High.

In a week they crossed the sound and reached the shore of Melville Island at Cape Hay. A hard journey had been made harder by fog and falling snow, in which they groped blindly among the hummocks, for Mr. Cresswell was unable to lay out an easy road for even the shortest distance ahead. The compass, too, was unreliable so near the magnetic pole; and though there was no danger of becoming lost with land so near before and behind, precious time and even more precious strength might be wasted by wandering off course. "Our chief recreation—our only encounter with living things—is with ptarmigan which migrate from Banks to Melville Island to spend the brief summer there. I have nine men in my tent, five of them too wretched to offer any assistance. They walk with difficulty behind the sledge, which the remaining four of us have to pull."

In the afternoon of April 23rd they camped for the first time on the shore of the long-sought Melville Island. Miertsching and three companions pitched the tent, and prepared a meal and beds for the five others who were scarcely more feeble than themselves. Weighed down as he was with cares and sickness, the German missionary found time to reflect with pride that Cape Hay had been Parry's "farthest" from the east thirty years before, and they had now, in spirit, joined hands with that great discoverer.

When all was done and our sick comrades made as snug as possible under their blankets, I felt the need of a little solitude. I quitted the tent and, in spite of my excessive fatigue, I climbed a little hill. There, seated on its summit, I surveyed the barren and desolate country. My eyes filled with tears, and, forgetting the cold, I fell into a profound reverie. I, Miertsching, who would never have thought myself destined to take part in an expedition to the Pole, have shared to some extent in the glory of the discovery which for three centuries has been attempted in vain! I returned to the tent shivering, but strengthened in spirit. My companions were asleep, and I ate my meal of sea-biscuit and salt meat alone.

It increases our respect for the brave German that, with all his devotion to religion and virtue, he responded just like other men to the charm of honour and glory.

For the next week they travelled up the shore of Melville Island, cheered by smoother ice and milder temperatures.

> The weather has been more favourable this week, but the increasing exhaustion of our comrades makes the journey most difficult.
>
> We have had to put two seamen on the sledges; others can keep going only by holding on to the sledge; and difficulties are aggravated by our two deranged comrades, who are a perpetual source of trouble. Whenever possible we march seven hours and then rest for five. Another march, and another stop of the same duration makes up the twenty-four hours. [Daylight was continuous by now.]

But they were nearing the end of the journey. On the morning of May 1st Mr. Cresswell, pioneering a road ahead, suddenly raised a shout that brought his comrades, sledges and all, scurrying up with feeble haste to join him. He passed his telescope around from man to man to give everyone a view of the bay fifteen miles away, where, clearly etched against the pale blue of the sky, rose the masts of the *Resolute* and *Intrepid*. The aroused men put on a spurt to finish the journey in one lap; but their strength was not equal to their spirit; they slowed down again and had to spend one more night camping on the snow.

The next day they rose early, and in a spirit of mutual goodwill offered apologies and received pardon for all the peevishness and ill-nature displayed on the journey. "We take breakfast happier and in a better humour than we have enjoyed for a long time. With emotion we have a short religious service, and upon rounding a rock we see the two ships. They, too, have seen us. They have hoisted a flag!" Figures were seen descending a ramp and hurrying over the ice towards them. Before long Captains Kellett and McClure and a handful of seamen were among them.

While the *Investigators* were exchanging greetings with these and asking questions about the homeland they had quitted forty months before, Kellett with instinctive courtesy came directly to the one stranger among them, shook hands with Miertsching, bade him welcome to the *Resolute,* and offered him the use of his cabin. Miertsching was soon revelling in the luxuries of the ship. "What a delight after sixteen days without being able to wash! They offer me hot coffee, real hot coffee. What a delight is this also! I have not tasted it for two and half years." Returning to his cabin after giving orders for the care of the new arrivals, Kellett found the poor interpreter stretched out in a profound sleep which lasted for several hours.

Kellett's two ships were almost deserted. His officers, Mc-Clintock and Mecham, Hamilton and Pim, were away with their main supporting parties exploring the west part of Melville Island and beyond, "partly as a work of scientific discovery, partly in the hope, now fast fading, of finding traces of Sir John Franklin." The *Intrepid* was converted into a hospital, and there not only the sick, but most of the supposedly sound men of Cresswell's party were placed under medical care.

Cresswell and Miertsching had themselves suffered too much to be deeply shocked by the effects of scurvy on others, but George McDougall was more sensitive; Macdonald, one of the *Investigators,* was, he wrote, "in a dreadful state; his flesh would retain an impression, if touched with the finger, like dough or putty; his legs were swollen to twice their natural size; whilst his teeth could be moved to and fro in their gums by the slightest movement of the tongue. He, however, recovered his health." With the journey over, the fittest men felt a painful reaction. "It is now," says Miertsching, "that we feel the full effects of our toilsome journey, and of sleeping on the snow. We have agonizing pains in our limbs. My right leg is so paralyzed that I can scarcely move it."

McClure, they learned, had been unable to alter Kellett's intentions about the desertion of the *Investigator.* Drs. Domville and Armstrong were appointed a board to examine the forty men who remained with her: if twenty of these, declared fit, would volunteer for the service, McClure could use them in a fresh effort to free his ship and bring her through the Passage. But unless these conditions were fulfilled, the ship must be abandoned. McClure returned to the Bay of Mercy in the faint hope of meeting these terms.

At the same time another departure took place. Kellett was anxious to get Wyniatt away with all possible speed in the hope that a change of scene might restore his reason. At the same time he gave Lieutenant Cresswell the honourable duty of carrying despatches to England with the news of the discovery of the Passage, which, though made nearly three years before, was still unknown to the civilized world. He therefore scraped together a sledge party from the few able men who remained on board, and put them under the command of the mate, Mr. Roche, with orders to take Cresswell and Wyniatt to the depot-ship *North Star*, whence they could get a passage to England on the summer supply ship.

"The departure of Lieutenant Cresswell has been unexpectedly hurried so that instead of writing at my ease, as it would seem one might do in a country where the postman is never in a hurry, I have been forced to write two letters under pressure. My pain did not make the task easier. I did not part without distress from Mr. Cresswell and poor Wyniatt, who stared at me with his great vacant eyes."

It does not appear that this gallant young officer ever recovered the use of his reason. Thirty years later Captain Collinson's biographer, when listing the names and subsequent fortunes of the officers of the *Enterprise* and *Investigator,* barely names Wyniatt, passing over his later career in silence.

Chapter fifteen

Trapped again in the ice

CRESSWELL AND Wyniatt reached England in October, and the former, after delivering his despatches, went to his home town of Lynn for celebrations in which the great Parry, who was living there in retirement, took part. Cresswell's services had been rewarded by a step in rank, and one can sympathize with the young man's pride and elation when greeted by the world-famous navigator, who had known him from boyhood, as "Captain Cresswell".

Like most of his comrades, Miertsching recovered rapidly with rest and full rations. Before long he is telling us:

> I am back from a week's hunting. We have bagged twenty-three ptarmigan and three caribou. Melville Island is dotted with little hills, the southern slopes of which are covered with turf. From the tops of these hills one sees a maze of little lakes. On our journey we frequently came across fragments of coal, weighing up to forty pounds, without being able to understand where they came from.

In early June Dr. Domville arrived back from the Bay of Mercy, reporting, as everyone expected, that the crew of the *Investigator* had, with one or two exceptions, been found unfit for service, and that the ship was to be deserted. Captain McClure "will be here next week with the rest of the crew, and our poor ship will remain in the ice. I cannot help remembering my plant and mineral collections."

17 June

This morning at a distance we made out the men of the *Investigator*. They approached so slowly that at noon they were still three miles away; and there was no means of going to their aid, for all our healthy men were away on sledge journeys. At 1 P.M. we met them with Captain Kellett to show them at least a mark of goodwill. They were a pitiful sight. The eight weakest were stretched two by two on sledges. Others were walking with their eyes on the ground, like moving corpses, dragged rather than supported by comrades who were almost as feeble as they. Those harnessed to the sledges were falling from fatigue every five minutes. The poor captain was going from one to another, aiding, exhorting, encouraging. Oh, indescribable misery! Then indeed we felt convinced that if the Good Lord had not sent us Lieutenant Pim, we would have perished on our journey to the last man.

The *Investigator* had been securely anchored; hatches and doors closed and nailed with the utmost care. All her provisions, food for seventy men for six months, were carried on shore. The captain, with all his regard for me, had not been able to bring my journal. Doubtless a few note-books would not have been too heavy; but he could not have done so without taking also the officers' journals, and that would have added too much to the weight of the sledges. Had I experienced a momentary feeling of disappointment, it would have been banished by a glance at those poor exhausted creatures. We gave them as good a reception as we could.

Dr. Armstrong appears to have smuggled through a piece of petrified wood which was later deposited in Dublin Museum; but possibly he had the captain's permission for this, as the specimen was of unusual interest and importance.

Miertsching made up as best he could for his disappointment by reconstructing his diary from memory with the aid of Mc-

Clure's journal, and betweentimes joined other officers in hunting to obtain fresh meat for the sick—musk-ox, caribou, and wild fowl. "We have not toiled in vain: most of the sick are regaining strength, and are helping to prepare the ship for departure."

A storehouse of immense strength was built on the shore, and in it were packed food, clothes, coal, and even books, in the faint hope that some of Franklin's men, still alive in that region, might benefit from them. Its whereabouts was marked by a tall mast, supported at its base by a cairn. The famous French-Canadian navigator of this century, Captain J. E. Bernier, visited this spot, and remarked on the infinite pains that Kellett took in this task, which none knew better than he to be all out hopeless.

It seemed more hopeless than ever after the middle of July. The last of the sledge travellers, Mecham and McClintock, came back from their respective journeys, which had brought to light two entirely new islands, Eglinton and Prince Patrick, without uncovering a trace of what they sought for. Supplied for ninety days, McClintock had stretched his journey to a hundred and five, by getting a little game, and had travelled a record fourteen hundred miles over a rough land and frozen sea. On the last stage of his journey back, "provision failed him and his crew; they had to abandon sledges, instruments and utensils to get to Dealy Island as quickly as possible. They ate only twice in the last three days, and, for lack of tents, slept in holes dug in the snow." It was not until 1915 that Vilhjalmur Stefansson carried discovery on beyond McClintock's farthest of 1853.

The hard winter of 1852-53 caused a correspondingly slow break-up of the ice in the next summer. Parry had broken out of Winter Harbour on August 1st; August 7th found Kellett's two ships locked in as fast as ever. A rift appeared in the seaward ice, and young Nares (later to win fame as a discoverer in both north and south polar regions) was sent with a boat and six men to scout eastward where the homeward route lay. "After three days they return shaking their heads and repeating despondently, 'Ice, nothing but ice!'" The *Investigators* began to have visions of spending a fourth winter as prisoners of the remorseless pack.

It was a trying time for both officers and men. All sledge journeys were over; the food depot had been built, packed, and secured; the ships were made ready for sea; and while the warm weather and bracing Arctic air invited activity, there was nothing to be done. But time seldom dragged for those who served under Henry Kellett; he got out fatigue parties, levelled an arena on the ice, and proclaimed the Dealy Island Sports Day. The men competed in the high jump, quoits, and racing while dragging loaded sledges. Mr. Nares won the hundred yards in fourteen seconds and the three hundred in forty-six; Kellett, slowed down by age but of great physical strength, took McClintock on his shoulders, ran fifty yards against Mr. Pim's hundred, and won by three yards. The officers bet freely, as if they were at Ascot, and set aside part of their winnings to furnish prizes for the men's events. It was probably the most northerly field day ever celebrated.

Temperatures continued high. "If the ice were only what it is in the severest German winter," observes Miertsching, "we would not have long to wait for its break-up in this weather. But with a thickness that ranges from six to fifteen feet it can only be broken by a tempest which stirs the sea to its depths."

On August 17th the tempest came. "A dull solemn rumbling is heard on all sides. Our ships, which are anchored to the ice, share in its tumultous heavings. The rudder and two boats of the *Intrepid* have been smashed like nutshells." As the storm continued they had an odd feeling that the land was in motion and receding; then they saw that the ice-sheet that had enclosed them for eleven months was in motion and driving out to sea. At last they were on the way home!

Clear of the land, they found themselves fenced in from navigable waters by the great floe to which they were still attached. The *Intrepid* was ordered to get up steam and tow them around this obstacle, when the floe began to "coach-wheel" and swung the two ships in a wide semicircle, with their heads pointing now this way and now that, into looser and more broken ice. By blasting and warping they got into the clear and once more rose and fell on the waves of the open sea. A number of men, especially the *Investigators,* long unused to such rhythm, became sea-sick.

They would have been happier had they remained at Dealy Island. The eastward drift of the ice into Barrow Strait was too rapid, and jammed up ahead of them. "North, south and east the ice has re-formed. To the west only does one perceive a navigable ocean, and our way lies to the east." The ships were again beset by ice, and drifted slowly on out of control. As they were near land—often too near, with the sea shoaling dangerously—parties went ashore from time to time and hunted the musk-ox with success.

Before the final utter disappointment they were mocked by one ray of hope.

> 10 September
>
> At daybreak the lookout shouts that there is no longer ice to the east. That way lies our route: Baffin Bay, Davis Strait, Europe, the Fatherland, all lie to the east. We sail all day. Faces are radiant. By the nightfall we find ourselves off the tip of Byam Martin Island, and anchor for the night for fear of the sand-bank which Captain Parry has reported hereabouts.

> 11 September
>
> We spent yesterday evening in counting the weeks and the days which separate us from our families.

Bets were freely laid as to the date of arrival in the Thames; some of the more arrogant and self-assertive were even challenging wagers as to the exact hour at which they would come to anchor. (Men change very little from one generation to the next, to be sure!) But it was mid-September, and though the old floes had dispersed, the young ice was beginning to form.

> Alas! at dawn great was our disappointment, when, after a still, cold night, we found ourselves surrounded by ice again, as far as the eye could reach. It is not thick; a breath of wind in our sails would send us crashing through this thin crust, but steam alone is not enough.

This phrase sounds odd in our days of ample power—a steam-tug requiring the aid of "a breath of wind" to become effective. In the afternoon the weather became overcast with heavy snow squalls from the north-north-west, and the ships began to forge ahead; but the young ice, not brittle but sludgy, gathered under the bows in sticky masses that small charges of powder could not wholly disperse. Fearing that in the gloomy weather he was being driven towards land, Kellett ordered sails taken in and the ships hove to. Nothing more could be done, and "we retired to rest," says McDougall, "amid the howling of the storm and grating of the ice, as the ship occasionally forged ahead, sounds which tended to lull us to sleep, much required by all."

The next day dawned stormy, with a few threads of water visible in ice-fields made tougher by the falling snow. Old ice to windward brought the *Resolute* under heavy pressure; it ploughed up the young ice as high as her gunwale, and heeled the ship over five degrees before easing off. The *Intrepid* was seen solidly fixed four hundred yards off. The two ships must winter in the pack without the shelter and chances of hunting that a landlocked harbour would have given them.

The hard trial of a fourth winter was made harder for the men of the *Investigator* by the discomforts of a ship on which they were extras, and where there was a shortage of both quarters and bedding. With the status of an officer, Miertsching found himself cabined in a little tarpaulin tent on the lower deck.

> We have no matresses; each bed consists of two covers, one brought with us; the other issued by the *Resolute*. . . . I do not sleep at night, and that could not last long were I not permitted to sleep by day in the officers' ward-room.

These hardships were cut short for one of the *Investigators*. The mate, Mr. Sainsbury, had developed tubercular symptoms shortly after leaving England, and had latterly grown so weak that Armstrong had not expected him to survive the journey on sledge from Mercy Bay to Dealy Island. An early return home might have prolonged his life; when hope of this was lost, his spirits drooped and the disease made rapid progress.

I had been much attached to him for four years. Dr. Piers and I spent much time with him during his illness, watching by his bedside and reading the Scriptures to him. Poor young man! How he sought, as the end drew near, to lay hold by faith on those Divine promises, to make them his own, during the dread passage from this world to the next. On the eve of his death he asked to see the captain and the officers; one after another he took leave of them, asking pardon for his faults and receiving from each a clasp of the hand in token of sympathy. To-morrow a large hole will be made in the ice to receive his body.

Poor fellow! [adds McDougall]. His body presented a dreadfully emaciated appearance. . . . On the 16th the few preparations required were completed; the funeral service was read on board, in a most impressive manner, by Captain Kellett, and the mournful procession then wended its way to the grave, a hole in the ice, about 250 yards from the ship. The day was cold (−20), and misty, and never shall I forget the scene on the ice, as the body, sewn in canvas, with weights attached, was launched through the narrow opening, and disappeared to our view. Within an hour, Nature had placed an icy slab over the grave of our departed messmate.

Chapter sixteen

The fourth winter—and the last

F
O R T W O weeks we have had nothing but gales and
blizzards. Impossible to quit the ship. We can only take
short turns on the deck in the space protected by the
housing. It is not enough; so we are very cold; for one
gets warm only by exercise. In other respects we are
better off than in previous winters. Rations, though reduced by one-third, are sufficient; artificial light is abundant; the numerous personnel of the ships gives more
importance to the element of sociability.

26 November

"The element of sociability" was not likely to be neglected
by any force under the command of Captain Kellett. Of their
own accord the men levelled an alley over the ice from one
ship to the other, and marked it with closely spaced pyramids to
provide shelter and guidance during a blizzard. To keep up com-
munications in the worst of weather, Lieutenant Hamilton in-
stalled what was then a great novelty, a telegraph line from the
Resolute to the *Intrepid.* "This invention has electrified our men.
They send all sorts of messages; they play chess by this medium."
(It would be interesting to know whether this was the first example of telegraphic chess in the history of the game.)

The telegraph proved its usefulness as soon as it was set up.
One night, two men of the *Intrepid* came aboard, covered with
drift and their whiskers buried in frost, to enquire after their
mate Hartnell, who was missing from his own ship. He proved
not to be on the *Resolute* either; and Kellett suggested that before searching parties were sent out Lieutenant Hamilton should

find out by wire if the missing man had returned during the interval.

A crowd gathered around while the operator spelt out—in less than a minute!—the enquiry, "Is Hartnell on board?" "A short time elapsed (this we expected, for of course the man must be sent for), when again the alarm sounded, and Y-E-S was read off with as much ease and facility as if Captain McClintock had personally responded to the enquiry." This communication with a ship less than a quarter of a mile away seemed almost marvellous a hundred years ago.

The telegraph was a standing joke with the men. When on a particularly foul night two *Intrepids* boarded the *Resolute* and one of them was asked: "Why, Jim, what the deuce brought you aboard on such a night as this 'ere?" he replied: "What brought me aboard? Why, I came over by the electric telegraph, to be sure." A roar of laughter greeted this "happy hit", and Kellett, overhearing it, rewarded the author with a glass of grog. One would have expected a higher standard of wit from an Irishman, but doubtless he thought that every attempt at promoting good cheer should be encouraged.

And so, without the radio and other comforts of modern polar stations, the winter was passed in comparative cheerfulness. A number of plays were staged, including *The Taming of the Shrew.* Perhaps Captain Kellett thus set a record in Shakespearian drama as he already had in field sports; for Parry, who had founded the Arctic "Theatre Royal" in 1819–20, had been less highbrow in his choice of entertainment. Mr Krabbé, master of the *Intrepid,* also gave displays of his skill as a conjuror. Miertsching, who as member of a small and strict sect knew less of artifical pleasures than the humblest seaman on board, was greatly astonished at these. A bystander tells us that when Mr. Krabbé gravely announced the marvel he was about to perform, Miertsching would throw out his arms with a frantic gesture and exclaim: "No! It is impossible. It cannot, cannot be!"

As a further useful pastime, the officers gave occasional lectures on the elements of astronomy, chemistry, and other sciences.

McDougall, with the superiority of the self-educated man, some-times doubted if these were properly understood by men of less learning than himself; Miertsching, who moved freely among all ranks, thought otherwise. The interest of the men, he said, was proved by the lectures becoming a common topic of conversation, and doing much to pass the time.

Nevertheless the severe winter, spent in the complete exposure of the bare and level sea, caused much sickness. By the New Year the hospital (on the *Intrepid*) was full to overflowing, and an extra ward was set up on the lower deck of the *Resolute* next to the tent which was Miertsching's cabin. He much appreciated the warmth of their stove, separated from him by a thick tar-paulin only, though he was disturbed by the groans of the sick.

> A poor marine among them does nothing but turn on his bed, full of groanings and self-pity. I have done much for him, testifying my sympathy and speaking to him of his Saviour. He could not endure me with patience, and finally commanded me to stay away. The doctor daily reads to him the prayers appointed in the Liturgy for the dangerously ill. He submits to that in silence, for he knows that that is according to Regulations, but his poor heart is, as it were, barricaded, and those solemn prayers seem to make not the least impression on him. At eleven o'clock, thinking to hear the death-rattle, I sprang up again to tell him for the last time of the love of Christ, but he lay rigid, and would not look at me. I could only kneel and commend him to the love of God. Towards two o'clock I could no longer hear anything; I got up again, but the sentry made a sign to me that all was over. He was a marine of the *Intrepid*.

While honouring Miertsching for his zeal and devotion, one could wish that he had not been so sure of his rightness as to force his beliefs on the dying marine until positively commanded to hold his tongue. As the old mate said, "The good ship *Victory* is a-sunk in the briny deep, and those who manned her, being good sailors and brave soldiers, are doubtless this moment in glory."

The poor marine (Thomas Hood by name) had been both a good sailor and a brave soldier. He had been the constant sledge-mate of McClintock on all his journeys, until the last, when the alert captain, detecting in him signs of weakening, had removed him from the crew and sent him back with the supporting sledge. Nor was his pity all for himself; some of it was for a bereaved sister. A few days before he died his captain had come over from the *Intrepid* to draw for him a will in which he bequeathed all that he had to her, except for a legacy of five pounds to his and McClintock's old sledge-mate, Shaw.

One of the finest stories in the history of the human race is the discovery in the last five hundred years of a New World of land and sea, by the seamen of western Europe in their old-fashioned sailing ships. The names of only a few leaders in this work are preserved; the hundreds of sailors who died by disease, famine, and shipwreck are forgotten. They are an army of unknown soldiers who died warring with savage nature. So let Thomas Hood be remembered as one of the few of a noble band whose name has been rescued from oblivion.

The zealous Miertsching was undiscouraged in his good work, and found the other two invalids readier to listen. But one of them also died, and the other was returned to the main hospital. "With them has disappeared my dear neighbour, the stove, by which I had been so agreeably indulged. The contrast is rude. When my servant brings hot water in the morning I have to hurry, for in a few minutes it freezes. It is difficult the little inconveniences in washing, and not the least of which perhaps is to dry one's face on a frost-hardened towel which burns the skin."

But winter was passing away, and with it the long period of inaction drew to an end. To relieve his overcrowded ships and save rations Kellett gave orders that in April the men of the *Investigator* should take to their sledges and travel to the depot-ship at Beechey Island, where abundant supplies awaited them.

The restored and reinvigorated crew received the news with joy. True, a tramp of a hundred and fifty miles in April was no joke, but it brought them that much nearer home, and from Beechey Island on, an open sea in summer was almost a certainty. "Once there we had no fear that the ice would again prove an impassable barrier to our homeward journey."

For other reasons they were not sorry to go. Relations among the crews were not too friendly. The *Investigators* no longer had any claim to sympathy, for most of them had grown well and fat at Dealy Island, while their rescuers were toiling on sledge journeys. An idle man, no matter how good his excuse, is not an agreeable sight to one who is forced to work. Inconvenient crowding during the winter had been one cause of annoyance. Another was the rules of conduct which Meirtsching had taught his shipmates.

> Our men have gained in a truly serious frame of mind. These noisy pleasures, the oaths, the equivocal songs, which the men of the *Resolute* make to resound in our ears remind me that it was once thus on the *Investigator*. Our long trials, our signal deliverance have borne fruit. I can say that our men have endured with Christian forbearance the scoff of their new comrades, and their biting remarks on the trouble and inconvenience we have caused them. They call us 'pietists'.

Kellett praised the *Investigators* for their good conduct while attached to his command, but he must have been glad to see them go.

They quitted the rescue ships on the 14th of April, and the tone of Miertsching's journal reflects the renewed vigour and elasticity of those who a year before had been on the brink of despair.

> Here we are . . . at the west side of the entrance of Wellington Channel. Everything is going better than we had dared to hope. The sledges are not too heavy; the

sailors are willing, overjoyed to be on the way home, and are supported by a sufficient ration. The route has been easy for the most part. From time to time, however, we have found the ice heaved up into little mountains forty-five feet high, which we have to climb over with great difficulty. The snow also, that fine dry snow into which the foot sinks seven or eight inches, becomes very fatiguing after a while. To offset this the weather has been fine, and the odd adventure has relieved the monotony of the journey.

The travellers were skirting the south shores of Bathurst and Cornwallis Islands, where, in the open tide-crack, the polar bear hunted the seal, and it was he who provided some of the adventures. One night the inmates of a tent were all snugly tucked away when a bear suddenly thrust his head in at the entrance. The tent commander snatched up his gun, but in bringing it to his shoulder let it off accidentally and broke the pole of the tent, which collapsed, enveloping in its folds the sleeping men and the bear, who was no less startled than they. The uproar aroused the men in the other tents, who came running up, shot the bear, and hauled out their comrades, who were the last to understand what was happening.

Some days later a similar thing happened in my tent. We had all gone to bed, snuggled one against the other, and buried up to our necks in our sleeping-bags. We were not yet asleep, and were listening to steps outside without much regarding them, for we thought it was some comrade coming in late. However a strange sort of heavy breathing made us listen intently, and through the carelessly fastened door of the tent we saw appearing the head and neck of a bear. A cool-headed seaman put an arm out of his bag and with his cutlass slashed an opening in the tent by which we got out, freeing ourselves, not without difficulty, from our sleeping-gear. We seized our guns, which lay loaded on the sledge, and the untimely guest soon fell pierced by several bullets. . . .

For my part I could relate a score of little happenings incidental to this life, which at a distance are a topic for mirth, but actually are anything but agreeable. Imagine one of us whose breath spread over his beard and the wool of his covering during the night and froze them firmly together. It is impossible to think of travelling with a sleeping-bag suspended from one's chin, and this is how we contrived to separate him from this awkward excrescence. His tent-mates lit their pipes and arranged themselves in a circle around their suffering comrade, and leaned forward so close to his chin that the warmth of the burning tobacco (which almost choked him) melted the ice and set his beard free.

Our boots which, wrapped in linen, serve as pillows are invariably found as stiff as an iron bar, and it is part of the morning routine to sit on them a certain time to restore flexibility, and enable them to be drawn on.

While this is going on the man appointed as cook has lighted the alcohol lamp outside the tent and put it under his kettle which is filled with ice or snow. As soon as it has melted he pours in powder of cocoa and sugar; then we bring our tin mugs and each one receives his portion of the beverage. But woe betide the one who is in a hurry and does not wait for the liquid to warm the cup! He brings it to his lips, and the skin remains attached to it pitilessly. All these incidents, and others like them, which can be imagined, were most often turned to mirth, and did not impair our good humour.

On April 28th they arrived at the *North Star,* berthed snugly between the perpendicular cliffs of Cape Riley and the rocky upheaval of Beechey Island offshore. Commander Pullen welcomed his visitors and made them as comfortable as possible. Miertsching, the universal handyman, took hammer and saw to help in the construction of cabins for himself and his brother officers on the upper deck.

When this work was finished he strolled a few hundred yards across the ice to Beechey Island. There on the beach were broken casks, glass, and fragments of cordage scattered here and there; in the background three graves marked by oaken slabs which bore the names and ages of the dead. There the *Erebus* and *Terror* had spent their first winter, 1845–46. Where they had gone from there was a mystery still unsolved.

Franklin's orders had directed him west along Barrow Strait, or north up Wellington Channel. Both those waterways had been thoroughly searched without result. No one imagined that he had found his way into the supposedly unnavigable Peel Sound to the south. To this day no one understands why no record was found at Beechey Island except the refuse of the winter quarters and the graves of those who died there. Franklin must have left a written notice of his intended course, but none has ever been found.

In crowded quarters, with at least two months with nothing to do, Miertsching was browned off, and painted a very gloomy picture of his surroundings:

> There can be nothing gloomier than the landscape which surround us. Certainly we have not been over-indulged that way since we entered Bering Strait. The regions which we have passed through have been nothing but a mournful blend of ice, rock, and snow; but here and there the southern slopes produce some vegetation, and, scanty as it is, this vegetation brings life to the scene by attracting the musk-ox, caribou, and other animals.
>
> Here there is nothing of the sort. It seems that up here the hundredth degree of longitude is a fatal line which vegetation does not cross. To the east of this line no words can express the spectacle—naked, stripped, and desolate—which meets the eye. Dark rocks, heaped

up in a disorder which is devoid of grandeur, in valleys of ice and snow. No verdure whatever, not even mosses or lichens; no living creatures except, in spring, a few white foxes in migration. Such is the picture of Barrow Strait.

The commander-in-chief of the expedition, Sir Edward Belcher, was fifty miles up Wellington Channel. His ships had been caught, like Kellett's, by early winter and frozen in. He resolved to abandon the ice-bound vessels, pack all five crews on the *North Star*, and quit the hopeless search. From the west and the north the liberated men came trooping in and took up quarters in huts at Cape Riley.

Kellett brought news that must have made McClure happier. He had sent Lieutenant Mecham and Mr. Krabbé back to Banks Land to look for traces of Collinson and his men. They learned from a record in Prince of Wales Strait that he was still safe, and able to take care of himself. Mr. Krabbé visited the Bay of Mercy and found the *Investigator* leaking and beginning to list and go down by the head. He was positive that water had not formed in the bay in the summer of 1853, so McClure saw that nothing had been lost by deserting her. He could not have got her out in any case.

The five crews assembled at Beechey Island were taking no chances of another winter's detention. They set to work with ice-saws and explosives, and cut or blasted a canal nine hundred feet long through ice fiften feet thick to the harbour entrance. The minds of the *Investigators* must have gone back to their own feeble efforts at Mercy Bay. Here it was different; there was plenty of strength for the work, and they were sure that the effort would not be wasted, for from the top of Beechey Island they could see to the south a moving sea, barely dotted with loose fragments of ice.

The jammed and bulging *North Star* had just quitted her anchorage when sails were reported on the horizon; the supply ships *Phoenix* and *Talbot* were approaching. Crews were re-distributed, and with the *Investigators* still on the *Star* they were off at last. Lancaster Sound was quite ice-free—soon they were sailing down Baffin Bay. Miertsching could not go too fast. On September 13, 1854, he notes:

> Towards evening we passed out of the Arctic Circle. We entered it in Bering Strait, 27 July, 1850. I hope that never again, as long as I live, shall I cross that fatal line!

The next day found them off Herrnhut, the site of the Moravian mission to the Greenland Eskimos. With all his impatience to be home, Miertsching wished to land and visit his fellow-workers, and Sir Edward Belcher, who treated him with great kindness, was ready to humour him; but the wind was blowing straight out of the bay, and they could not wait for it to change. They soon rounded Cape Farewell, the south end of Greenland:

> We travel rapidly without meeting the least ice. After the last few years such navigation seems the most extravagant of luxuries; but the nearer we approach home, the more uncontrollable grows the yearning to be there. . . .
>
> In the last few days we have been meeting ships in increasing numbers, sailing in all directions. We see distant lighthouses and a bluish line which they tell me is the Irish coast. . . . This evening the lights of the little town of Hastings (Sussex) are in distant view. It is time to give one's self a less savage appearance. I have begun by cutting off my beard, which for four years no razor has touched.

After so many years of delay and frustration, everything was coming their way. When the wind failed them off the Thames an Admiralty tug approached and took them in tow.

> A radiant sun has just risen. We are going up the Thames. Our eyes, wearied with endless expanses of ice

and snow, rest with delight on tree-dotted meadows, and on farm cattle which recall by contrast the savage eyes of the musk-ox. I cannot describe what I feel: since July 4, 1850, we have not seen a green tree. These cultivated fields, these houses, this stir of activity, *this life,* which one sees on all sides, what a spectacle it furnishes! How many times during our exile have we sighed for these things! How often we have feared that we would never see them again! I do not think that anyone could conceive our emotion, our joy, our wonder. No one thought of eating and drinking.

Chapter seventeen

The homecoming

TOWARDS NIGHTFALL they came to anchor. Miertsching could be a jolly companion when it fitted the occasion. Finding himself in the English harbour which for so many years had been the object of his hopes and prayers, he did not assemble his little flock of sailors for a service of thanksgiving. Instead, feeling a craving for two commodities of which he had long been deprived, he pooled his money with that of other officers to send ashore for fresh vegetables and beer.

They banquetted happily that evening. The *Investigator's* officers were not of his "little flock", but they were men who could honour manhood in another, though under a quaint exterior. With cheerful talk and good-fellowship they made felt their respect for the queer, talkative German missionary so strangely planted in their midst five years before, and on the morrow to be parted from them forever.

The newspapers had announced the arrival of the *North Star,* and the next morning found the dock crowded with the wives of officers and men, with their children. Not all of these found a happy reunion.

> In the midst of their pure family joys, in the midst of their hugging, embracing, and rapturous outcries, there were the bitterest tears. Poor women had come full of hope with children clinging to them to whom during the long years of separation they had always talked of their father. Alas! that father, that husband, lies far away in his lonely and icy tomb. And the heart-broken widow goes away clasping her bereaved orphans to her. God console and sustain them!

An Admiralty order was now read to the *Investigators,* expressed in the most flattering language, but giving the unpleasant news that their reunion with their families could not be made permanent, nor could leave be granted, until a court martial had made formal enquiry into the loss of their ship. Miertsching at once wrote pointing out that he had had no part in the handling of the vessel, and asking for an immediate discharge; it was granted. His little congregation of sailors saw him off at the railway station and he was gone. "I have enjoyed the kindness, the esteem, and latterly the affection of almost all the officers and men," he wrote in his journal, and there is no doubt that the claim was well founded.

The *Investigators* were acquitted by court martial of losing their ship through neglect, and later they received the thanks of Parliament and a generous monetary reward for their discoveries. The men who had rescued and nursed them back to health got nothing but the double pay to which all Arctic volunteers were entitled. The loyal Kellett was hurt at this, and declared that he would gladly contribute fifty pounds towards a fund for rewarding the men of the *Resolute* and *Intrepid* whose services had been unnoticed by Parliament. But the brave fellows themselves bore no grudge; when McClintock took command of the *Fox* in the last, and only successful, expedition to search for news of Franklin, he was able to enlist seventeen old comrades in a crew of twenty-five.

It was not until the next spring, in 1855, that Collinson and his *Enterprise* arrived home. He had spent three whole years in the Arctic, and had been away in all five years and four months, yet he brought ship and men home in excellent trim. He was one of the best, and quite the unluckiest, of the arctic captains of the period. In 1852 he had, with a skill that amazed those who came after him, taken his ship through the shallow and treacherous Dolphin and Union Strait to the now well-known station of Cambridge Bay. There he wintered within two hundred miles of the actual scene of Franklin's disaster. It was his plan to search both sides of Victoria Strait, but when spring came he found the ice so rough that he was obliged to keep his two parties together so that crews could help one another in easing the heavily loaded sledges over the hummocks. In consequence he searched the west side of the strait only.

Years later he had the cruel mortification of learning that had he gone over to the east side he would have discovered Franklin's fate and achieved the success that he deserved so well. His disappointment was made more bitter by the thought that if he had had Miertsching with him he would have learned of the disaster from the Eskimos of Victoria Island and have been directed to the right spot. So he paid dearly for his good-nature in leaving the German interpreter on the *Investigator*.

And what *had* happened to Franklin and his two ships? Up to a point their story is the same as that of the *Investigator*. Just like McClure, they had gone through an unknown strait, Peel Sound, and off King William Island had found the last link in the Northwest Passage in the ice-choked waters of Victoria Strait. Like the *Investigators*, they had remained there ice-bound for two winters. But there was no *Resolute* at hand to give them aid. Franklin died, and his sick and starving crews, finding their ships solidly fixed, tried to escape southwards on foot—just as the *Investigators* intended to do. At first one by one, and then in numbers, they dropped off; the last survivors barely reached the Canadian mainland, where they died huddled together under an upturned boat in a little inlet, Starvation Cove. Years afterwards, Dr. Rae of the Hudson's Bay Company learned of the disaster from Eskimo friends. On his report, Captain Leopold McClintock was sent out in the *Fox* to find the expedition's records, and learn exactly what had happened. He found only a few skeletons, an abandoned boat, and one short written record. From this it was learnt that Franklin's ships had, like the *Investigator*, been permanently locked in the ice. The old sailor had died, and his starving crews had quitted the ships and tramped off to the south with very faint hopes of reaching the Hudson's Bay Company posts a thousand miles away. That, with the little information he could gather from the Eskimos of the region, makes up most of what we know today of the tragic cruise of the *Erebus* and the *Terror*.

McClure and his men had penetrated so deeply into the Arctic, so far ahead of the march of civilization, that for a long time their discoveries were neglected and almost forgotten. American whalers, who came in towards the end of the century, knew the south shore of Banks Land only, and the famous landmark of Nelson Head. When Amundsen in 1903–06 took his little *Gjoa* through the Northwest Passage, he followed not McClure's route, but Franklin's—with one improvement, suggested by McClintock.

Then the Canadian Government took over the islands from Great Britain, and began to roll back the frontier. In 1909–10 Captain Bernier of the C.G.S. *Arctic* based himself at Winter Harbour and sent a party over to Mercy Bay. In 1914 Vilhjalmur Stefansson, sturdiest and most resourceful of arctic travellers, came over the Beaufort Sea, feeding himself on seal and polar bear, and drifting on an ice-cake. He reached land to the south of Ballast Beach, and set up his base at Sachs Harbour, inside the cape that McClure had named after the good old Kellett. From there he set out to discover new islands far to the north of the farthest of McClintotck.

In 1944 Staff Sergeant (now Superintendent) H. A. Larsen of the RCMP took his *St. Roch* in by Barrow Strait, crossed the hitherto impassable Melville Sound, and went through Prince of Wales Strait to complete the Northwest Passage by the route of the old *Investigator*. In his opinion this route is the only one for larger ships.

Support was given to Larsen's opinion by the 1954 voyage of the Canadian Navy ice-breaker, HMCS *Labrador*. She sailed up from Halifax through Lancaster Sound to Dealy Island, and turning her head to the south-west, crossed Melville Sound in four days, crunching and shouldering her way through ice blocks twenty feet thick at the rate of thirty miles a day. From there she had a fairly easy passage through Prince of Wales Strait, the Beaufort Sea, and Bering Strait, down to Vancouver. Thence she sailed back to Halifax by way of the Panama Canal, putting a belt around the North American continent.

Today oil companies are applying for exploration permits on both sides of the Bay of Mercy. It is no fanciful vision that sees ships, mines, oil wells, and all the badges of a wealthy and luxurious civilization where a century back Miertsching and his shipmates struggled desperately for survival against hunger, darkness and cold.

BIBL. J.N. DESMARAIS LIBR.

3 0007 00506270 7